# LOW CARB
# HIGH PROTEIN
# COOKBOOK
## FOR BEGINNERS

*Barbara Grey*

**2024 EDITION**

**Disclaimer**

This book provides information for educational and informational purposes. The author and the publisher are not responsible for any consequences resulting from the use of the information contained herein. It is advisable to consult a qualified professional for any health, legal, or financial-related matters. The use of the information in this book is at your own risk.

# TABLE OF CONTENT

## DINNER                                              39

# Welcome

Welcome to "Low Carb High Protein Cookbook for Beginners!" This book is your gateway to embracing a healthier lifestyle through delicious, nutritious meals that are easy to prepare. Whether you're completely new to low-carb, high-protein diets or looking to refine your current eating habits, this cookbook is designed to guide you on a transformative journey towards better health. Our goal is to help you lose weight, build muscle, and enjoy every meal without feeling deprived or overwhelmed.

In today's fast-paced world, it can be challenging to find the time and resources to maintain a healthy diet. That's why this book focuses on providing quick, easy, and flavorful recipes that fit seamlessly into your busy life. With a comprehensive 60-day meal plan and a variety of recipes, you'll have everything you need to make lasting changes to your diet and health. We're here to make sure that healthy eating is both convenient and enjoyable, offering practical tips and insights to support you every step of the way.

## Benefits of Low-Carb, High-Protein Diets [1]

Low-carb, high-protein diets have become increasingly popular for their effectiveness in promoting weight loss, improving muscle mass, and enhancing overall health. These diets focus on reducing carbohydrate intake while increasing protein consumption, offering a variety of benefits backed by scientific research.

### Weight Loss

One of the primary benefits of low-carb, high-protein diets is weight loss. Studies have shown that reducing carbohydrate intake can lead to significant weight loss, particularly in the initial stages. A landmark study published in the New England Journal of Medicine found that participants on a low-carb diet lost more weight than those on a traditional low-fat diet over a six-month period . This weight loss is largely attributed to a reduction in appetite and increased satiety, which helps individuals consume fewer calories overall.

### Increased Satiety and Reduced Appetite

High-protein diets are known to increase feelings of fullness, which can help reduce overall calorie intake. Protein has a high thermic effect, meaning it requires more energy to digest compared to fats and carbohydrates. This leads to increased energy expenditure and can help with weight management. Research published in the American Journal of Clinical Nutrition demonstrated that high-protein diets can significantly reduce hunger and appetite, leading to lower calorie consumption throughout the day .

## Improved Muscle Mass and Strength

Protein is essential for muscle repair and growth. By increasing protein intake, individuals can support muscle synthesis, especially when combined with resistance training. A study in the Journal of the International Society of Sports Nutrition highlighted that higher protein intake, along with resistance exercise, led to greater increases in muscle mass and strength compared to lower protein diets . This is particularly beneficial for individuals looking to build or maintain muscle mass while losing fat.

## Enhanced Metabolic Health

Low-carb, high-protein diets have been shown to improve several markers of metabolic health, including blood sugar levels, insulin sensitivity, and lipid profiles. Reducing carbohydrate intake can help stabilize blood sugar levels, which is particularly beneficial for individuals with type 2 diabetes or insulin resistance. A study in Diabetes Care found that low-carb diets improved glycemic control and reduced the need for diabetes medication in patients with type 2 diabetes .

## Cardiovascular Health

While there has been some debate about the long-term effects of low-carb diets on heart health, several studies suggest that these diets can improve cardiovascular risk factors. Research published in the Annals of Internal Medicine found that low-carb diets were more effective at reducing cardiovascular risk factors, such as triglycerides and blood pressure, compared to low-fat diets (MuscleandStrength). Additionally, high-protein diets can help reduce levels of LDL cholesterol (often referred to as "bad" cholesterol) and increase HDL cholesterol (the "good" cholesterol).

## Improved Mental Clarity and Focus

Many individuals report improved mental clarity and focus when following a low-carb, high-protein diet. This may be due to the stabilization of blood sugar levels and the reduction of blood sugar spikes and crashes that can occur with high-carb diets. A study in Physiology & Behavior suggested that lower carbohydrate intake might positively influence cognitive function and mood .

*Sustainable Eating Habits*

Adopting a low-carb, high-protein diet can lead to more sustainable eating habits. By focusing on whole, unprocessed foods and reducing the intake of refined carbohydrates and sugars, individuals can develop a healthier relationship with food. This approach to eating emphasizes nutrient-dense foods, which can lead to improved overall health and well-being.

## How This Book Can Help You

This book offers a comprehensive 60-day meal plan and a variety of recipes that are both easy to make and delicious. Whether you prefer following a structured plan or experimenting with new recipes, you'll find everything you need to achieve your health and fitness goals. Our meal plan and recipes are designed to fit into your busy lifestyle, ensuring that healthy eating is both convenient and enjoyable for you and your family.

## Understanding Macronutrients: Carbs, Proteins, and Fats

Understanding the role of macronutrients is crucial for any dietary plan. Carbohydrates are the body's primary energy source, but excessive intake can lead to weight gain and metabolic issues. Proteins are essential for building and repairing tissues, making them vital for muscle growth and recovery. Fats, especially healthy fats, are important for hormone production, brain function, and energy. Balancing these macronutrients can optimize your health and help you reach your fitness goals.

## Setting Your Goals: Weight Loss and Muscle Gain

Setting realistic and achievable goals is the first step towards success. Whether you aim to lose a specific amount of weight, build muscle, or improve overall fitness, having clear objectives helps keep you motivated and focused. Track your progress regularly, adjust your plan as needed, and celebrate your achievements along the way.

[1] Key Studies and Resources

Samaha, F. F., et al. (2003). A Low-Carbohydrate as Compared with a Low-Fat Diet in Severe Obesity. New England Journal of Medicine, 348(21), 2074-2081.

Weigle, D. S., et al. (2005). A high-protein diet induces sustained reductions in appetite, ad libitum caloric intake, and body weight despite compensatory changes in diurnal plasma leptin and ghrelin concentrations. American Journal of Clinical Nutrition, 82(1), 41-48.

Morton, R. W., et al. (2018). A systematic review, meta-analysis, and meta-regression of the effect of protein supplementation on resistance training-induced gains in muscle mass and strength in healthy adults. Journal of the International Society of Sports Nutrition, 15(1), 26.

Westman, E. C., et al. (2008). The effect of a low-carbohydrate, ketogenic diet versus a low-glycemic index diet on glycemic control in type 2 diabetes mellitus. Nutrition & Metabolism, 5(1), 36.

Bazzano, L. A., et al. (2014). Effects of low-carbohydrate and low-fat diets: a randomized trial. Annals of Internal Medicine, 161(5), 309-318.

Brinkworth, G. D., et al. (2009). Long-term effects of a very low-carbohydrate diet and a low-fat diet on mood and cognitive function. Archives of Internal Medicine, 169(20), 1873-1880.

# Getting Started

## *Essential Kitchen Tools and Gadgets*

To ensure a smooth and enjoyable cooking experience, it's important to have the right tools and gadgets in your kitchen. Here are some essentials that will make preparing low-carb, high-protein meals easier:

**Quality Knives:** A good chef's knife and a paring knife are essential for chopping and slicing ingredients efficiently.

**Cutting Board:** Use a sturdy cutting board to prepare your ingredients safely.

**Blender/Food Processor:** Ideal for making smoothies, sauces, and purees.

**Measuring Cups and Spoons:** Accurate measurements are crucial for recipe success.

**Mixing Bowls:** A set of various sizes will come in handy for mixing ingredients.

**Non-Stick Skillets and Pans:** Perfect for cooking without using too much oil.

**Baking Sheets:** Essential for roasting vegetables and baking low-carb treats.

**Slow Cooker/Instant Pot:** Great for making meals with minimal effort.

**Kitchen Scale:** Helps with portion control and accurate ingredient measurements.

**Storage Containers:** Keep your meals fresh and make meal prep easier with good-quality containers.

## *Pantry Staples for Low-Carb, High-Protein Cooking*

Stocking your pantry with the right ingredients ensures you're always ready to create healthy meals. Here are some staples to keep on hand:

**Proteins:** Chicken breast, turkey, lean beef, fish, eggs, tofu, and tempeh.

**Vegetables:** Leafy greens, broccoli, cauliflower, zucchini, bell peppers, and avocados.

**Healthy Fats:** Olive oil, coconut oil, avocado oil, nuts, and seeds.

**Low-Carb Flours:** Almond flour, coconut flour, and flaxseed meal.

**Herbs and Spices:** Basil, oregano, thyme, garlic powder, onion powder, paprika, and black pepper.

**Dairy and Alternatives:** Greek yogurt, cottage cheese, almond milk, and cheese.

**Canned Goods:** Tuna, salmon, tomatoes, and beans (in moderation).

**Condiments:** Mustard, hot sauce, soy sauce, vinegar, and sugar-free dressings.

*Tips for Meal Planning and Preparation*

Effective meal planning and preparation can save you time and help you stick to your dietary goals. Here are some tips to get started:

*Plan Your Meals*

Take some time each week to plan your meals. Decide what you'll have for breakfast, lunch, dinner, and snacks.

*Make a Grocery List*

Write down all the ingredients you'll need for your meal plan. Stick to your list when shopping to avoid impulse buys.

*Prep in Batches*

Set aside a few hours each week to prep your meals. Cook large batches of proteins, chop vegetables, and prepare sauces.

*Use Leftovers*

Incorporate leftovers into your meal plan to reduce waste and save time.

*Stay Organized*

Keep your pantry and fridge organized so you can easily find ingredients.

## How to Use This Book

This cookbook is designed to be user-friendly and flexible.
Here's how to make the most of it:

**Explore the Recipes:** Feel free to browse through the recipes and choose ones that appeal to you. Each recipe is designed to be easy, tasty, and healthy.

**Follow the Meal Plan:** If you prefer a structured approach, follow the 60-day meal plan. It provides a comprehensive guide to eating low-carb, high-protein meals for two months.

**Customize to Your Needs:** Adjust the recipes and meal plan to suit your dietary needs and preferences. Substitute ingredients as needed and modify portion sizes based on your goals.

**Track Your Progress:** Use the tips and tools provided to track your progress. Keep a food journal, take measurements, and celebrate your successes.

# BREAKFAST

# GREEK YOGURT PARFAIT WITH BERRIES & NUTS

**SERVINGS:** 4          **PREP. TIME:** 10 min.          **COOK TIME:** none

## INGREDIENTS

- 2 cups plain Greek yogurt

- 1 cup mixed berries (strawberries, blueberries, raspberries)

- ¼ cup chopped nuts (almonds, walnuts)

- 1 tablespoon honey (optional)

## STEPS

1. In a bowl, layer ½ cup of Greek yogurt.

2. Add a layer of mixed berries.

3. Sprinkle with chopped nuts.

4. Repeat the layers.

5. Drizzle with honey if desired.

**NUTRITIONAL INFORMATIONS (PER SERVING):** 220 Calories, 20g. Proteins, 12g. Carbohydrates, 10g. Fats.

# SPINACH & FETA OMELETTE

**SERVINGS:** 4          **PREP. TIME:** 15 min.          **COOK TIME:** 10 min.

## INGREDIENTS

- 8 large eggs

- 1 cup fresh spinach, chopped

- ½ cup feta cheese, crumbled

- ¼ cup milk (optional)

- Salt and pepper to taste

- 1 tablespoon olive oil

## STEPS

1. In a bowl, whisk together the eggs, milk, salt, and pepper.

2. Heat olive oil in a non-stick pan over medium heat.

3. Pour the egg mixture into the pan.

4. Add spinach and feta cheese evenly over the eggs.

5. Cook until the eggs are set, then fold the omelette in half.

**NUTRITIONAL INFORMATIONS (PER SERVING):** 220 Calories, 18g. Proteins, 4g. Carbohydrates, 14g. Fats.

# AVOCADO & SMOKED SALMON TOAST

**SERVINGS:** 4      **PREP. TIME:** 10 min.      **COOK TIME:** 5 min.

## INGREDIENTS

- 4 slices whole-grain bread

- 2 ripe avocados, mashed

- 8 oz smoked salmon

- 1 tablespoon lemon juice

- Salt and pepper to taste

- Optional: red pepper flakes, fresh dill

## STEPS

1. Toast the whole-grain bread slices.

2. In a bowl, mix mashed avocados with lemon juice, salt, and pepper.

3. Spread the avocado mixture on each toast.

4. Top with smoked salmon slices.

5. Garnish with red pepper flakes and fresh dill if desired.

**NUTRITIONAL INFORMATIONS (PER SERVING):** 300 Calories, 15g. Proteins, 20g. Carbohydrates, 18g. Fats.

# COTTAGE CHEESE WITH BERRIES & ALMONDS

**SERVINGS:** 4      **PREP. TIME:** 5 min.      **COOK TIME:** none

## INGREDIENTS

- 2 cups cottage cheese

- 1 cup mixed berries (strawberries, blueberries, raspberries)

- ¼ cup sliced almonds

- 1 teaspoon honey (optional)

## STEPS

1. Divide cottage cheese into four bowls.

2. Top with mixed berries and sliced almonds.

3. Drizzle with honey if desired.

**NUTRITIONAL INFORMATIONS (PER SERVING):** 180 Calories, 15g. Proteins, 10g. Carbohydrates, 8g. Fats.

# Scrambled Eggs with Spinach & Tomatoes

**SERVINGS:** 4      **PREP. TIME:** 10 min.      **COOK TIME:** 10 min.

## INGREDIENTS

- 8 large eggs

- 1 cup fresh spinach, chopped

- 1 cup cherry tomatoes, halved

- ¼ cup milk (optional)

- Salt and pepper to taste

- 1 tablespoon butter

## STEPS

1. In a bowl, whisk together the eggs, milk, salt, and pepper.

2. Heat butter in a non-stick pan over medium heat.

3. Add spinach and cherry tomatoes, and cook for 2 minutes.

4. Pour in the egg mixture and cook, stirring, until scrambled.

**NUTRITIONAL INFORMATIONS (PER SERVING):** 230 Calories, 18g. Proteins, 4g. Carbohydrates, 15g. Fats.

# Chia Seed Pudding with Almond Milk & Berries

**SERVINGS:** 4      **PREP. TIME:** 10 min.      **COOK TIME:** none

## INGREDIENTS

- ¼ cup chia seeds

- 1 cup almond milk

- 1 teaspoon vanilla extract

- 1 tablespoon honey or maple syrup

- ½ cup mixed berries

## STEPS

1. In a bowl, mix chia seeds, almond milk, vanilla extract, and honey.

2. Stir well and **refrigerate overnight**.

3. In the morning, stir the pudding and top with mixed berries.

**NUTRITIONAL INFORMATIONS (PER SERVING):** 180 Calories, 5g. Proteins, 18g. Carbohydrates, 9g. Fats.

# Egg Muffins

**SERVINGS:** 4     **PREP. TIME:** 10 min.     **COOK TIME:** 25 min.

## INGREDIENTS

- 8 large eggs
- ½ cup diced bell peppers
- ½ cup chopped spinach
- ¼ cup diced onions
- ¼ cup shredded cheese
- Salt and pepper to taste

## STEPS

1. Preheat oven to 350°F (175°C).
2. In a bowl, whisk the eggs, salt, and pepper.
3. Mix in the vegetables and cheese.
4. Pour the mixture into a greased muffin tin.
5. Bake for 20-25 minutes or until eggs are set.

**NUTRITIONAL INFORMATIONS (PER SERVING):** 120 Calories, 10g. Proteins, 2g. Carbohydrates, 8g. Fats.

# Oats with Almond Butter & Bananas

**SERVINGS:** 4     **PREP. TIME:** 10 min.     **COOK TIME:** none

## INGREDIENTS

- 1 cup rolled oats
- 1 cup almond milk
- 2 tablespoons almond butter
- 1 banana, sliced
- 1 teaspoon chia seeds

## STEPS

1. In a jar, combine oats, almond milk, almond butter, and chia seeds.
2. Stir well, cover, and ***refrigerate overnight***.
3. In the morning, top with sliced bananas.

**NUTRITIONAL INFORMATIONS (PER SERVING):** 250 Calories, 8g. Proteins, 30g. Carbohydrates, 10g. Fats.

# HAM & CHEESE ROLL-UPS

**SERVINGS:** 4      **PREP. TIME:** 10 min.      **COOK TIME:** 10 min.

## INGREDIENTS

- 8 slices ham

- 4 slices cheese (cheddar or Swiss)

- 1 tablespoon mustard (optional)

- ¼ cup chopped green onions

## STEPS

1. Preheat oven to 350°F (175°C).

2. Place a slice of cheese on each ham slice.

3. Roll up tightly and place on a baking sheet.

4. Bake for 10 minutes or until cheese is melted.

5. Garnish with chopped green onions and mustard if desired.

**NUTRITIONAL INFORMATIONS (PER SERVING):** 150 Calories, 12g. Proteins, 2g. Carbohydrates, 8g. Fats.

# PROTEIN PANCAKES

**SERVINGS:** 4      **PREP. TIME:** 10 min.      **COOK TIME:** 15 min.

## INGREDIENTS

- 1 cup rolled oats

- 1 cup cottage cheese

- 4 large eggs

- 1 teaspoon vanilla extract

- 1 teaspoon baking powder

- 1 tablespoon coconut oil

## STEPS

1. Blend oats in a blender until finely ground.

2. Add cottage cheese, eggs, vanilla extract, and baking powder. Blend until smooth.

3. Heat coconut oil in a non-stick pan over medium heat.

4. Pour batter into the pan and cook until bubbles form on the surface. Flip and cook until golden brown.

**NUTRITIONAL INFORMATIONS (PER SERVING):** 220 Calories, 20g. Proteins, 12g. Carbohydrates, 8g. Fats.

# BURRITOS

**SERVINGS:** 4      **PREP. TIME:** 10 min.      **COOK TIME:** 10 min.

## INGREDIENTS

- 4 whole-grain tortillas
- 8 large eggs
- ½ cup diced bell peppers
- ½ cup diced onions
- ½ cup shredded cheese
- ¼ cup salsa
- Salt and pepper to taste

## STEPS

1. In a bowl, whisk eggs with salt and pepper.
2. Heat a non-stick pan over medium heat and cook the eggs until scrambled.
3. Warm the tortillas in a separate pan.
4. Divide the eggs, bell peppers, onions, and cheese among the tortillas.
5. Roll up the tortillas and serve with salsa.

**NUTRITIONAL INFORMATIONS (PER SERVING):** 240 Calories, 18g. Proteins, 15g. Carbohydrates, 12g. Fats.

# SAUSAGE & EGG SKILLET

**SERVINGS:** 4      **PREP. TIME:** 10 min.      **COOK TIME:** 15 min.

## INGREDIENTS

- 8 large eggs
- ½ pound sausage (chicken or turkey)
- 1 cup bell peppers, diced
- 1 cup onions, diced
- 1 cup spinach, chopped
- ¼ cup shredded cheese
- Salt and pepper to taste

## STEPS

1. Cook sausage in a non-stick pan over medium heat until browned.
2. Add bell peppers and onions, and cook for 5 minutes.
3. In a bowl, whisk eggs with salt and pepper.
4. Add eggs and spinach to the pan, and cook until eggs are set.
5. Top with shredded cheese before serving.

**NUTRITIONAL INFORMATIONS (PER SERVING):** 280 Calories, 20g. Proteins, 7g. Carbohydrates, 18g. Fats.

# Turkey Bacon & Egg Cups

**SERVINGS:** 4          **PREP. TIME:** 10 min.          **COOK TIME:** 20 min.

## INGREDIENTS

- 8 slices turkey bacon
- 8 large eggs
- ½ cup diced bell peppers
- ¼ cup chopped spinach
- Salt and pepper to taste

## STEPS

1. Preheat oven to 350°F (175°C).
2. Line a muffin tin with turkey bacon slices to form cups.
3. Crack an egg into each bacon cup.
4. Sprinkle with diced bell peppers and spinach.
5. Season with salt and pepper.
6. Bake for 15-20 minutes or until eggs are set.

**NUTRITIONAL INFORMATIONS (PER SERVING):** 180 Calories, 16g. Proteins, 2g. Carbohydrates, 10g. Fats.

# Low-Carb Pizza

**SERVINGS:** 4          **PREP. TIME:** 10 min.          **COOK TIME:** 10 min.

## INGREDIENTS

- 4 low-carb tortillas
- 8 large eggs
- ½ cup shredded cheese
- ½ cup diced tomatoes
- ¼ cup sliced olives
- ¼ cup chopped green onions
- ¼ cup chopped spinach
- 1 tablespoon olive oil
- Salt and pepper to taste

## STEPS

1. Preheat oven to 375°F (190°C).
2. Place tortillas on a baking sheet.
3. In a bowl, whisk eggs with salt and pepper.
4. Heat olive oil in a non-stick pan and scramble the eggs.
5. Spread scrambled eggs evenly over the tortillas.
6. Top with shredded cheese, diced tomatoes, olives, green onions, and spinach.
7. Bake for 10 minutes or until cheese is melted and tortillas are crispy.

**NUTRITIONAL INFORMATIONS (PER SERVING):** 250 Calories, 20g. Proteins, 8g. Carbohydrates, 14g. Fats.

# Salmon & Asparagus Frittata

**SERVINGS:** 4     **PREP. TIME:** 10 min.     **COOK TIME:** 20 min.

## INGREDIENTS

- 8 large eggs
- 1 cup cooked salmon, flaked
- 1 cup asparagus, chopped
- ¼ cup milk (optional)
- ¼ cup shredded cheese
- Salt and pepper to taste
- 1 tablespoon olive oil

## STEPS

1. Preheat oven to 375°F (190°C).
2. In a bowl, whisk eggs, milk, salt, and pepper.
3. Heat olive oil in an oven-safe skillet over medium heat.
4. Add asparagus and cook for 3-4 minutes.
5. Add salmon and pour the egg mixture over.
6. Sprinkle with cheese and transfer skillet to the oven.
7. Bake for 15-20 minutes or until eggs are set.

**NUTRITIONAL INFORMATIONS (PER SERVING):** 280 Calories, 22g. Proteins, 5g. Carbohydrates, 18g. Fats.

# Coconut Flour Waffles

**SERVINGS:** 4     **PREP. TIME:** 10 min.     **COOK TIME:** 10 min.

## INGREDIENTS

- ½ cup coconut flour
- 4 large eggs
- ¼ cup melted coconut oil
- 1 cup almond milk
- 1 teaspoon vanilla extract
- 1 teaspoon baking powder

## STEPS

1. Preheat waffle iron.
2. In a bowl, mix coconut flour, baking powder, and salt.
3. In another bowl, whisk eggs, coconut oil, almond milk, and vanilla extract.
4. Combine wet and dry ingredients.
5. Pour batter into waffle iron and cook until golden brown.

**NUTRITIONAL INFORMATIONS (PER SERVING):** 180 Calories, 10g. Proteins, 6g. Carbohydrates, 14g. Fats.

# ALMOND BUTTER PROTEIN BARS

**SERVINGS:** 4      **PREP. TIME:** 10 min.      **COOK TIME:** none

## INGREDIENTS

- 1 cup almond butter

- ½ cup almond flour

- ¼ cup protein powder (vanilla or chocolate)

- 2 tablespoons erythritol or preferred sweetener

- 1 teaspoon vanilla extract

- ¼ cup dark chocolate chips (optional)

## STEPS

1. In a bowl, mix almond butter, almond flour, protein powder, sweetener, and vanilla extract.

2. Fold in dark chocolate chips if using.

3. Press mixture into a lined baking dish.

4. Refrigerate for at least 2 hours before cutting into bars.

**NUTRITIONAL INFORMATIONS (PER SERVING):** 250 Calories, 12g. Proteins, 8g. Carbohydrates, 20g. Fats.

# KETO CHOCOLATE CHIP PANCAKES

**SERVINGS:** 4      **PREP. TIME:** 10 min.      **COOK TIME:** 15 min.

## INGREDIENTS

- 1 cup almond flour

- ¼ cup coconut flour

- 1 teaspoon baking powder

- ¼ cup sugar-free chocolate chips

- 4 large eggs

- 1 cup almond milk

- 1 teaspoon vanilla extract

- 1 tablespoon coconut oil

## STEPS

1. In a bowl, mix almond flour, coconut flour, and baking powder.

2. In another bowl, whisk eggs, almond milk, and vanilla extract.

3. Combine wet and dry ingredients, then fold in chocolate chips.

4. Heat coconut oil in a non-stick pan over medium heat.

5. Pour batter into the pan and cook until bubbles form. Flip and cook until golden brown.

**NUTRITIONAL INFORMATIONS (PER SERVING):** 250 Calories, 12g. Proteins, 8g. Carbohydrates, 18g. Fats.

# CINNAMON ROLL MUG CAKE

**SERVINGS:** 4     **PREP. TIME:** 5 min.     **COOK TIME:** 2 min.

## INGREDIENTS

- ¼ cup almond flour
- 1 tablespoon coconut flour
- ½ teaspoon baking powder
- ¼ teaspoon cinnamon
- 1 large egg
- 2 tablespoons almond milk
- 1 tablespoon melted coconut oil
- 1 tablespoon erythritol or preferred sweetener
- ½ teaspoon vanilla extract

## STEPS

1. In a mug, mix all dry ingredients.

2. Add egg, almond milk, coconut oil, and vanilla extract. Mix well.

3. Microwave for 1-2 minutes or until cooked through.

**NUTRITIONAL INFORMATIONS (PER SERVING):** 150 Calories, 8g. Proteins, 6g. Carbohydrates, 12g. Fats.

# LOW-CARB QUESADILLA

**SERVINGS:** 4     **PREP. TIME:** 10 min.     **COOK TIME:** 10 min.

## INGREDIENTS

- 4 low-carb tortillas
- 8 large eggs
- 1 cup shredded cheese
- ½ cup diced bell peppers
- ½ cup diced onions
- 1 avocado, sliced
- Salsa (optional)
- Salt and pepper to taste

## STEPS

1. In a bowl, whisk the eggs with salt and pepper.

2. Heat a non-stick pan and cook the eggs until scrambled.

3. Place tortillas in a separate pan, sprinkle with cheese, and add scrambled eggs, bell peppers, and onions.

4. Fold the tortillas in half and cook until cheese is melted.

5. Serve with avocado slices and salsa.

**NUTRITIONAL INFORMATIONS (PER SERVING):** 280 Calories, 20g. Proteins, 10g. Carbohydrates, 15g. Fats.

# LUNCH

# GRILLED CHICKEN CAESAR SALAD

**SERVINGS:** 4      **PREP. TIME:** 10 min.      **COOK TIME:** 10 min.

## INGREDIENTS

- 2 grilled chicken breasts, sliced
- 1 head romaine lettuce, chopped
- ¼ cup grated Parmesan cheese
- ½ cup Caesar dressing (low-carb)
- ½ cup cherry tomatoes, halved
- ¼ cup croutons (optional, for low-carb use almond flour croutons)

## STEPS

1. In a large bowl, combine romaine lettuce, cherry tomatoes, and Parmesan cheese.
2. Add grilled chicken slices on top.
3. Drizzle with Caesar dressing and toss gently to coat.
4. Add croutons if desired.

**NUTRITIONAL INFORMATIONS (PER SERVING):** 320 Calories, 30g. Proteins, 8g. Carbohydrates, 20g. Fats.

# TURKEY AVOCADO WRAP

**SERVINGS:** 4      **PREP. TIME:** 10 min.      **COOK TIME:** none

## INGREDIENTS

- 8 slices turkey breast
- 2 avocados, sliced
- 4 large low-carb tortillas
- ½ cup shredded lettuce
- ¼ cup mayonnaise
- ¼ cup Dijon mustard
- Salt and pepper to taste

## STEPS

1. In a small bowl, mix mayonnaise and Dijon mustard.
2. Spread the mixture evenly over the tortillas.
3. Layer turkey slices, avocado slices, and shredded lettuce on each tortilla.
4. Season with salt and pepper.
5. Roll up tightly and cut in half to serve.

**NUTRITIONAL INFORMATIONS (PER SERVING):** 280 Calories, 20g. Proteins, 10g. Carbohydrates, 18g. Fats.

# BAKED SALMON WITH DILL & LEMON

**SERVINGS:** 4      **PREP. TIME:** 10min.      **COOK TIME:** 20 min.

## INGREDIENTS

- 4 salmon fillets

- 2 tablespoons olive oil

- 1 lemon, sliced

- 2 tablespoons fresh dill, chopped

- Salt and pepper to taste

## STEPS

1. Preheat oven to 375°F (190°C).

2. Place salmon fillets on a baking sheet.

3. Drizzle with olive oil, then top with lemon slices and dill.

4. Season with salt and pepper.

5. Bake for 15-20 minutes or until salmon is cooked through.

**NUTRITIONAL INFORMATIONS (PER SERVING):** 290 Calories, 25g. Proteins, 3g. Carbohydrates, 15g. Fats.

# EGGPLANT LASAGNA

**SERVINGS:** 4      **PREP. TIME:** 15 min.      **COOK TIME:** 30 min.

## INGREDIENTS

- 2 large eggplants, sliced lengthwise

- 1 pound ground beef

- 1 cup marinara sauce (low-carb)

- 1 cup ricotta cheese

- 1 cup shredded mozzarella cheese

- ¼ cup grated Parmesan cheese

- 1 tablespoon olive oil

- Salt and pepper to taste

## STEPS

1. Preheat oven to 375°F (190°C).

2. Brush eggplant slices with olive oil and bake for 10 minutes until tender.

3. In a pan, cook ground beef until browned. Add marinara sauce and simmer for 10 minutes.

4. In a baking dish, layer eggplant slices, beef mixture, ricotta cheese, and mozzarella cheese.

5. Repeat layers and top with Parmesan cheese.

6. Bake for 25-30 minutes until cheese is melted and bubbly.

**NUTRITIONAL INFORMATIONS (PER SERVING):** 380 Calories, 30g. Proteins, 12g. Carbohydrates, 25g. Fats.

# Shrimp & Avocado Salad

**SERVINGS:** 4     **PREP. TIME:** 10 min.     **COOK TIME:** 5 min.

## INGREDIENTS

- 1 pound shrimp, cooked and peeled
- 2 avocados, diced
- ¼ cup red onion, finely chopped
- ¼ cup cilantro, chopped
- 2 tablespoons lime juice
- Salt and pepper to taste

## STEPS

1. In a large bowl, combine shrimp, avocados, red onion, and cilantro.

2. Drizzle with lime juice and toss gently to combine.

3. Season with salt and pepper to taste.

**NUTRITIONAL INFORMATIONS (PER SERVING):** 280 Calories, 25g. Proteins, 6g. Carbohydrates, 18g. Fats.

# Grilled Chicken & Pesto Wrap

**SERVINGS:** 4     **PREP. TIME:** 10 min.     **COOK TIME:** 6 min.

## INGREDIENTS

- 2 grilled chicken breasts, sliced
- 4 large low-carb tortillas
- ¼ cup pesto sauce
- ½ cup shredded mozzarella cheese
- ½ cup roasted red peppers, sliced
- ¼ cup fresh basil leaves

## STEPS

1. Spread pesto sauce evenly over the tortillas.

2. Layer grilled chicken, mozzarella cheese, roasted red peppers, and basil leaves on each tortilla.

3. Roll up tightly and grill for 2-3 minutes on each side until cheese is melted.

**NUTRITIONAL INFORMATIONS (PER SERVING):** 350 Calories, 28g. Proteins, 12g. Carbohydrates, 20g. Fats.

# CHICKEN & VEGETABLE SKEWERS

**SERVINGS:** 4     **PREP. TIME:** 15 min.     **COOK TIME:** 12 min.

## INGREDIENTS

- 2 grilled chicken breasts, diced
- 1 red bell pepper, diced
- 1 yellow bell pepper, diced
- 1 zucchini, sliced
- 1 red onion, diced
- ¼ cup olive oil
- 2 tablespoons lemon juice
- 2 cloves garlic, minced
- Salt and pepper to taste

## STEPS

1. In a bowl, mix olive oil, lemon juice, garlic, salt, and pepper.
2. Thread chicken, bell peppers, zucchini, and onion onto skewers.
3. Brush skewers with the marinade.
4. Grill over medium heat for 10-12 minutes, turning occasionally, until chicken is cooked through and vegetables are tender.

**NUTRITIONAL INFORMATIONS (PER SERVING):** 250 Calories, 25g. Proteins, 10g. Carbohydrates, 12g. Fats.

# SPAGHETTI SQUASH WITH MEATBALLS

**SERVINGS:** 4     **PREP. TIME:** 20 min.     **COOK TIME:** 40 min.

## INGREDIENTS

- 1 large spaghetti squash
- 1 pound ground beef
- ½ cup grated Parmesan cheese
- ¼ cup almond flour
- 1 egg
- 2 cups marinara sauce (low-carb)
- 1 tablespoon olive oil
- 1 teaspoon Italian seasoning
- Salt and pepper to taste

## STEPS

1. Preheat oven to 375°F (190°C). Cut spaghetti squash in half, remove seeds, and brush with olive oil.
2. Bake squash halves face down on a baking sheet for 40 minutes until tender.
3. In a bowl, mix ground beef, Parmesan cheese, almond flour, egg, Italian seasoning, salt, and pepper.
4. Form meatballs and place on a baking sheet. Bake for 20 minutes until cooked through.
5. In a pan, heat marinara sauce and add cooked meatballs.
6. Use a fork to scrape out the spaghetti squash strands and serve with meatballs and sauce.

**NUTRITIONAL INFORMATIONS (PER SERVING):** 320 Calories, 28g. Proteins, 10g. Carbohydrates, 18g.Fats.

# Kale & Quinoa Salad

**SERVINGS:** 4  **PREP. TIME:** 10 min.  **COOK TIME:** 10 min.

## INGREDIENTS

- 2 cups kale, chopped
- 1 cup cooked quinoa
- ½ cup cherry tomatoes, halved
- ¼ cup red onion, thinly sliced
- ¼ cup feta cheese, crumbled
- ¼ cup olive oil
- 2 tablespoons lemon juice
- Salt and pepper to taste

## STEPS

1. In a large bowl, combine kale, quinoa, cherry tomatoes, red onion, and feta cheese.

2. In a small bowl, whisk together olive oil, lemon juice, salt, and pepper.

3. Pour dressing over the salad and toss gently to combine.

**NUTRITIONAL INFORMATIONS (PER SERVING):** 250 Calories, 10g. Proteins, 15g. Carbohydrates, 18g. Fats.

# Tuna Avocado Sandwich

**SERVINGS:** 4  **PREP. TIME:** 10 min.  **COOK TIME:** none

## INGREDIENTS

- 2 cans tuna, drained
- 2 avocados, mashed
- ¼ cup red onion, finely chopped
- ¼ cup celery, diced
- 1 tablespoon lemon juice
- Salt and pepper to taste
- 8 slices low-carb bread

## STEPS

1. In a large bowl, combine tuna, mashed avocados, red onion, celery, lemon juice, salt, and pepper.

2. Mix well until all ingredients are evenly combined.

3. Spread the mixture onto 4 slices of bread and top with the remaining slices to form sandwiches.

**NUTRITIONAL INFORMATIONS (PER SERVING):** 260 Calories, 20g. Proteins, 8g. Carbohydrates, 18g. Fats.

# SPICY SHRIMP LETTUCE WRAPS

**SERVINGS:** 4     **PREP. TIME:** 10 min.     **COOK TIME:** 5 min.

## INGREDIENTS

- 1 pound cooked shrimp, peeled and deveined
- 8 large lettuce leaves (such as romaine or butter lettuce)
- ¼ cup mayonnaise
- 1 tablespoon sriracha sauce
- ¼ cup shredded carrots
- ¼ cup sliced cucumber

## STEPS

1. In a small bowl, mix mayonnaise and sriracha sauce.
2. Spread the mixture evenly over the lettuce leaves.
3. Layer cooked shrimp, shredded carrots, and cucumber slices on each leaf.
4. Roll up tightly and serve.

**NUTRITIONAL INFORMATIONS (PER SERVING):** 200 Calories, 20g. Proteins, 4g. Carbohydrates, 12g. Fats.

# ZUCCHINI NOODLES WITH PESTO & CHICKEN

**SERVINGS:** 4     **PREP. TIME:** 10 min.     **COOK TIME:** 10 min.

## INGREDIENTS

- 4 zucchinis, spiralized
- 2 grilled chicken breasts, sliced
- ½ cup pesto sauce
- ¼ cup cherry tomatoes, halved
- ¼ cup grated Parmesan cheese

## STEPS

1. Heat a pan over medium heat and sauté zucchini noodles for 3-4 minutes until tender.
2. Add grilled chicken slices and cherry tomatoes to the pan.
3. Stir in pesto sauce and cook for another 2 minutes.
4. Serve topped with grated Parmesan cheese.

**NUTRITIONAL INFORMATIONS (PER SERVING):** 280 Calories, 24g. Proteins, 7g. Carbohydrates, 18g. Fats.

# ASIAN CHICKEN SALAD

**SERVINGS:** 4      **PREP. TIME:** 10 min.      **COOK TIME:** 10 min.

## INGREDIENTS

- 2 grilled chicken breasts, sliced
- 4 cups mixed salad greens
- 1 cup shredded carrots
- 1 cup shredded red cabbage
- ½ cup sliced almonds
- ¼ cup green onions, sliced
- ¼ cup sesame dressing (low-carb)

## STEPS

1. In a large bowl, combine salad greens, shredded carrots, shredded cabbage, sliced almonds, and green onions.
2. Add grilled chicken slices on top.
3. Drizzle with sesame dressing and toss gently to combine.

**NUTRITIONAL INFORMATIONS (PER SERVING):** 280 Calories, 28g. Proteins, 8g. Carbohydrates, 18g. Fats.

# EGGPLANT & HUMMUS WRAP

**SERVINGS:** 4      **PREP. TIME:** 10 min.      **COOK TIME:** 10 min.

## INGREDIENTS

- 1 large eggplant, sliced and grilled
- 1 cup hummus
- 4 large low-carb tortillas
- ½ cup shredded lettuce
- ¼ cup red onion, thinly sliced
- ¼ cup roasted red peppers, sliced
- Salt and pepper to taste

## STEPS

1. Spread hummus evenly over the tortillas.
2. Layer grilled eggplant slices, shredded lettuce, red onion, and roasted red peppers on each tortilla.
3. Season with salt and pepper.
4. Roll up tightly and cut in half to serve.

**NUTRITIONAL INFORMATIONS (PER SERVING):** 220 Calories, 10g. Proteins, 15g. Carbohydrates, 10g. Fats.

# BEEF & VEGETABLE STIR-FRY

**SERVINGS:** 4      **PREP. TIME:** 10 min.      **COOK TIME:** 10 min.

## INGREDIENTS

- 1 pound beef sirloin, thinly sliced
- 2 cups broccoli florets
- 1 red bell pepper, sliced
- 1 yellow bell pepper, sliced
- ½ cup snow peas
- 2 tablespoons soy sauce (low-sodium)
- 1 tablespoon sesame oil
- 2 cloves garlic, minced
- 1 tablespoon fresh ginger, minced
- 1 tablespoon sesame seeds

## STEPS

1. Heat sesame oil in a large pan over medium-high heat.

2. Add garlic and ginger, and cook for 1 minute.

3. Add beef and cook until browned, about 3-4 minutes.

4. Add broccoli, bell peppers, and snow peas, and cook for another 5 minutes.

5. Stir in soy sauce and cook for an additional 2 minutes.

6. Sprinkle with sesame seeds before serving.

**NUTRITIONAL INFORMATIONS (PER SERVING):** 320 Calories, 28g. Proteins, 10g. Carbohydrates, 18g. Fats.

# TURKEY & CRANBERRY WRAP

**SERVINGS:** 4      **PREP. TIME:** 10 min.      **COOK TIME:** none

## INGREDIENTS

- 8 slices turkey breast
- 4 large low-carb tortillas
- ½ cup cranberry sauce (sugar-free)
- ¼ cup cream cheese
- ½ cup shredded lettuce
- Salt and pepper to taste

## STEPS

1. Spread cream cheese evenly over the tortillas.

2. Layer turkey slices, cranberry sauce, and shredded lettuce on each tortilla.

3. Season with salt and pepper.

4. Roll up tightly and cut in half to serve.

**NUTRITIONAL INFORMATIONS (PER SERVING):** 280 Calories, 20g. Proteins, 12g. Carbohydrates, 15g. Fats.

# Salmon Avocado Salad

**SERVINGS:** 4      **PREP. TIME:** 10 min.      **COOK TIME:** 5 min.

## INGREDIENTS

- 2 cups cooked salmon, flaked
- 2 avocados, diced
- 4 cups mixed salad greens
- ½ cup cherry tomatoes, halved
- ¼ cup red onion, finely chopped
- ¼ cup olive oil
- 2 tablespoons lemon juice
- Salt and pepper to taste

## STEPS

1. In a large bowl, combine salad greens, cherry tomatoes, red onion, and flaked salmon.
2. Add diced avocado on top.
3. In a small bowl, whisk together olive oil, lemon juice, salt, and pepper.
4. Drizzle dressing over the salad and toss gently to combine.

**NUTRITIONAL INFORMATIONS (PER SERVING):** 320 Calories, 25g. Proteins, 5g. Carbohydrates, 22g. Fats.

# Chicken & Veggie Wrap

**SERVINGS:** 4      **PREP. TIME:** 10 min.      **COOK TIME:** 10 min.

## INGREDIENTS

- 2 grilled chicken breasts, sliced
- 4 large low-carb tortillas
- ½ cup shredded lettuce
- ½ cup shredded carrots
- ½ cup sliced cucumber
- ¼ cup Greek yogurt
- 1 tablespoon lemon juice
- Salt and pepper to taste

## STEPS

1. In a small bowl, mix Greek yogurt and lemon juice.
2. Spread the mixture evenly over the tortillas.
3. Layer grilled chicken slices, shredded lettuce, shredded carrots, and cucumber slices on each tortilla.
4. Season with salt and pepper.
5. Roll up tightly and cut in half to serve.

**NUTRITIONAL INFORMATIONS (PER SERVING):** 260 Calories, 24g. Proteins, 12g. Carbohydrates, 12g. Fats.

# BAKED COD WITH GARLIC & HERB BUTTER

**SERVINGS:** 4 **PREP. TIME:** 10 min. **COOK TIME:** 20 min.

## INGREDIENTS

- 4 cod fillets

- ¼ cup butter, melted

- 2 cloves garlic, minced

- 2 tablespoons fresh parsley, chopped

- 1 tablespoon lemon juice

- Salt and pepper to taste

## STEPS

1. Preheat oven to 375°F (190°C).

2. Place cod fillets in a baking dish.

3. In a small bowl, mix melted butter, garlic, parsley, lemon juice, salt, and pepper.

4. Pour the mixture over the cod fillets.

5. Bake for 15-20 minutes or until fish is opaque and flakes easily with a fork.

**NUTRITIONAL INFORMATIONS (PER SERVING):** 240 Calories, 25g. Proteins, 2g. Carbohydrates, 15g. Fats.

# MEDITERRANEAN TUNA SALAD

**SERVINGS:** 4 **PREP. TIME:** 10 min. **COOK TIME:** none

## INGREDIENTS

- 2 cans tuna, drained

- ¼ cup red onion, finely chopped

- ¼ cup Kalamata olives, pitted and halved

- ¼ cup cherry tomatoes, halved

- ¼ cup feta cheese, crumbled

- 2 tablespoons olive oil

- 2 tablespoons lemon juice

- 1 teaspoon dried oregano

- Salt and pepper to taste

## STEPS

1. In a large bowl, combine tuna, red onion, olives, cherry tomatoes, and feta cheese.

2. In a small bowl, whisk together olive oil, lemon juice, oregano, salt, and pepper.

3. Pour dressing over the salad and toss gently to combine.

**NUTRITIONAL INFORMATIONS (PER SERVING):** 250 Calories, 20g. Proteins, 5g. Carbohydrates, 15g. Fats.

# DINNER

# GRILLED STEAK WITH CHIMICHURRI SAUCE

SERVINGS: 4     PREP. TIME: 15 min.     COOK TIME: 10 min.

## INGREDIENTS

- 4 steaks (sirloin, ribeye, or your choice)
- 1 cup fresh parsley
- ¼ cup fresh cilantro
- 2 cloves garlic
- ¼ cup red wine vinegar
- ½ cup olive oil
- 1 teaspoon red pepper flakes
- Salt and pepper to taste

## STEPS

1. Preheat grill to medium-high heat.

2. Season steaks with salt and pepper.

3. Grill steaks for 4-5 minutes on each side or until desired doneness.

4. In a food processor, combine parsley, cilantro, garlic, red wine vinegar, red pepper flakes, salt, and pepper. Blend until smooth.

5. With the processor running, slowly add olive oil until well combined.

6. Serve steaks with chimichurri sauce.

NUTRITIONAL INFORMATIONS (PER SERVING): 370 Calories, 28g. Proteins, 4g. Carbohydrates, 25g. Fats.

# BAKED LEMON HERB SALMON

SERVINGS: 4     PREP. TIME: 10 min.     COOK TIME: 20 min.

## INGREDIENTS

- 4 salmon fillets
- 2 tablespoons olive oil
- 1 lemon, sliced
- 1 tablespoon fresh dill, chopped
- 1 tablespoon fresh parsley, chopped
- Salt and pepper to taste

## STEPS

1. Preheat oven to 375°F (190°C).

2. Place salmon fillets on a baking sheet lined with parchment paper.

3. Drizzle olive oil over salmon and top with lemon slices, dill, parsley, salt, and pepper.

4. Bake for 15-20 minutes or until salmon is cooked through and flakes easily with a fork.

NUTRITIONAL INFORMATIONS (PER SERVING): 290 Calories, 25g. Proteins, 3g. Carbohydrates, 15g. Fats.

# BALSAMIC GLAZED CHICKEN

**SERVINGS:** 4 | **PREP. TIME:** 10 min. | **COOK TIME:** 15 min.

## INGREDIENTS

- 4 boneless, skinless chicken breasts
- ¼ cup balsamic vinegar
- 2 tablespoons honey
- 2 cloves garlic, minced
- 2 tablespoons olive oil
- Salt and pepper to taste
- Fresh basil, chopped (for garnish)

## STEPS

1. In a small bowl, mix balsamic vinegar, honey, garlic, salt, and pepper.

2. Heat olive oil in a large skillet over medium-high heat. Add chicken breasts and cook for 5-7 minutes on each side until cooked through.

3. Pour balsamic mixture over chicken and cook for an additional 2-3 minutes, allowing the glaze to thicken.

4. Garnish with fresh basil before serving.

**NUTRITIONAL INFORMATIONS (PER SERVING):** 280 Calories, 28g. Proteins, 10g. Carbohydrates, 12g.Fats.

# LEMON GARLIC SHRIMP PASTA

**SERVINGS:** 4 | **PREP. TIME:** 10 min. | **COOK TIME:** 10 min.

## INGREDIENTS

- 1 pound shrimp, peeled and deveined
- 4 zucchinis, spiralized into noodles
- ¼ cup butter
- 4 cloves garlic, minced
- 1 lemon, juiced and zested
- ¼ cup grated Parmesan cheese
- Fresh parsley, chopped (for garnish)
- Salt and pepper to taste

## STEPS

1. Melt butter in a large skillet over medium heat. Add garlic and cook for 1 minute.

2. Add shrimp and cook until pink, about 3-4 minutes.

3. Stir in lemon juice, lemon zest, salt, and pepper.

4. Add zucchini noodles and cook for 2-3 minutes until tender.

5. Serve with grated Parmesan cheese and garnish with fresh parsley.

**NUTRITIONAL INFORMATIONS (PER SERVING):** 280 Calories, 25g. Proteins, 6g. Carbohydrates, 18g. Fats.

# Spicy Turkey & Zucchini Skillet

SERVINGS: 4      PREP. TIME: 10 min.      COOK TIME: 20 min.

## INGREDIENTS

- 2 pounds ground turkey
- 4 garlic cloves, minced
- 1 onion, chopped
- 2 bell peppers, chopped
- 4 zucchinis, sliced into half-moons
- 2 teaspoons chili powder
- 1 teaspoon paprika
- 1 teaspoon cumin
- 1/2 teaspoon red pepper flakes (optional)
- 1 cup shredded cheddar or mozzarella cheese (optional)
- Salt and pepper to taste
- 2 tablespoons olive oil

## STEPS

1. Heat 1 tablespoon olive oil in a large skillet. Add the ground turkey, chili powder, paprika, cumin, salt, and pepper. Cook until browned, then set aside.

2. In the same skillet, add the remaining 1 tablespoon olive oil, minced garlic, chopped onion, and bell peppers. Sauté until soft. Add the zucchini slices and cook until tender.

3. Return the turkey to the skillet, mix well with the vegetables. Sprinkle 1 cup of shredded cheese on top, cover, and let it melt for 1 to 2 minutes.

4. Serve hot, optionally garnished with fresh herbs like parsley or cilantro.

NUTRITIONAL INFORMATIONS (PER SERVING): 400 Calories, 45g. Proteins, 10g. Carbohydrates, 20g. Fats.

# Garlic Butter Shrimp with Asparagus

SERVINGS: 4      PREP. TIME: 10 min.      COOK TIME: 15 min.

## INGREDIENTS

- 1 pound shrimp, peeled and deveined
- 1 pound asparagus, trimmed and cut into pieces
- 4 tablespoons butter
- 4 cloves garlic, minced
- 1 lemon, juiced
- Salt and pepper to taste
- Fresh parsley, chopped (for garnish)

## STEPS

1. In a large skillet, melt 2 tablespoons butter over medium heat. Add garlic and cook for 1 minute.

2. Add shrimp and cook until pink, about 3-4 minutes. Remove from skillet and set aside.

3. In the same skillet, melt the remaining butter. Add asparagus and cook until tender, about 5-7 minutes.

4. Return shrimp to the skillet and add lemon juice. Cook for an additional 2 minutes.

5. Season with salt and pepper, and garnish with fresh parsley before serving.

NUTRITIONAL INFORMATIONS (PER SERVING): 280 Calories, 25g. Proteins, 6g. Carbohydrates, 18g. Fats.

# LAMB CHOPS WITH MINT YOGURT SAUCE

**SERVINGS:** 4          **PREP. TIME:** 10 min.          **COOK TIME:** 10 min.

## INGREDIENTS

- 8 lamb chops
- 2 tablespoons olive oil
- 2 cloves garlic, minced
- 1 teaspoon dried rosemary
- 1 cup Greek yogurt
- 1/4 cup fresh mint, chopped
- 1 tablespoon lemon juice
- Salt and pepper to taste

## STEPS

1. Preheat grill to medium-high heat.

2. In a small bowl, mix olive oil, garlic, rosemary, salt, and pepper. Rub mixture over lamb chops.

3. Grill lamb chops for 4-5 minutes on each side until desired doneness.

4. In a separate bowl, mix Greek yogurt, mint, lemon juice, salt, and pepper.

5. Serve lamb chops with mint yogurt sauce.

**NUTRITIONAL INFORMATIONS (PER SERVING):** 340 Calories, 30g. Proteins, 4g. Carbohydrates, 20g. Fats.

# GARLIC PARMESAN CRUSTED PORK CHOPS

**SERVINGS:** 4          **PREP. TIME:** 10 min.          **COOK TIME:** 20 min.

## INGREDIENTS

- 4 boneless pork chops
- ½ cup grated Parmesan cheese
- ½ cup almond flour
- 1 teaspoon garlic powder
- 1 teaspoon dried parsley
- 2 tablespoons olive oil
- Salt and pepper to taste

## STEPS

1. Preheat oven to 375°F (190°C).

2. In a bowl, combine Parmesan cheese, almond flour, garlic powder, parsley, salt, and pepper.

3. Dredge each pork chop in the mixture, pressing to adhere.

4. Heat olive oil in a large oven-safe skillet over medium-high heat. Cook pork chops for 2-3 minutes on each side until golden.

5. Transfer skillet to the oven and bake for 15-20 minutes until pork chops are cooked through.

**NUTRITIONAL INFORMATIONS (PER SERVING):** 350 Calories, 30g. Proteins, 6g. Carbohydrates, 22g. Fats.

# CREAMY TUSCAN GARLIC CHICKEN

| SERVINGS: 4 | PREP. TIME: 10 min. | COOK TIME: 20 min. |
|---|---|---|

## INGREDIENTS

- 4 boneless, skinless chicken breasts
- 2 tablespoons olive oil
- ½ cup sun-dried tomatoes, chopped
- 1 cup heavy cream
- ½ cup chicken broth
- 3 cloves garlic, minced
- ½ cup grated Parmesan cheese
- 2 cups fresh spinach
- Salt and pepper to taste

## STEPS

1. Heat olive oil in a large skillet over medium-high heat.
2. Season chicken breasts with salt and pepper, and cook for 5-7 minutes on each side until golden and cooked through. Remove from skillet and set aside.
3. In the same skillet, add garlic and sun-dried tomatoes, and cook for 1 minute.
4. Stir in heavy cream, chicken broth, and Parmesan cheese. Bring to a simmer.
5. Add spinach and cook until wilted.
6. Return chicken to the skillet and simmer for an additional 5 minutes.

**NUTRITIONAL INFORMATIONS (PER SERVING):** 350 Calories, 30g. Proteins, 8g. Carbohydrates, 25g. Fats.

# CAJUN CHICKEN & CAULIFLOWER RICE

| SERVINGS: 4 | PREP. TIME: 10 min. | COOK TIME: 20 min. |
|---|---|---|

## INGREDIENTS

- 4 boneless, skinless chicken breasts
- 1 tablespoon Cajun seasoning
- 2 tablespoons olive oil
- 1 head cauliflower, grated into rice-sized pieces
- 1 red bell pepper, diced
- 1 green bell pepper, diced
- 1 small onion, diced
- 2 cloves garlic, minced
- Salt and pepper to taste

## STEPS

1. Season chicken breasts with Cajun seasoning.
2. Heat olive oil in a large skillet over medium-high heat. Cook chicken for 5-7 minutes on each side until cooked through. Remove and set aside.
3. In the same skillet, add bell peppers, onion, and garlic. Cook for 3-4 minutes.
4. Add cauliflower rice and cook for another 5 minutes until tender.
5. Slice chicken and serve over cauliflower rice mixture.

**NUTRITIONAL INFORMATIONS (PER SERVING):** 280 Calories, 30g. Proteins, 10g. Carbohydrates, 15g. Fats.

# SAUSAGE & PEPPERS

**SERVINGS:** 4      **PREP. TIME:** 10 min.      **COOK TIME:** 20 min.

## INGREDIENTS

- 1 pound Italian sausage (mild or hot)
- 1 red bell pepper, sliced
- 1 green bell pepper, sliced
- 1 yellow bell pepper, sliced
- 1 onion, sliced
- 2 cloves garlic, minced
- 2 tablespoons olive oil
- ¼ cup chicken broth
- 1 teaspoon dried oregano
- Salt and pepper to taste

## STEPS

1. Heat olive oil in a large skillet over medium-high heat.
2. Add sausages and cook until browned on all sides. Remove from skillet and set aside.
3. In the same skillet, add garlic, onion, and bell peppers. Cook until tender, about 5-7 minutes.
4. Slice the sausages and return to the skillet.
5. Add chicken broth and oregano, and cook for an additional 5 minutes until sausages are cooked through.
6. Season with salt and pepper before serving.

**NUTRITIONAL INFORMATIONS (PER SERVING):** 300 Calories, 20g. Proteins, 8g. Carbohydrates, 22g. Fats.

# TERIYAKI SALMON

**SERVINGS:** 4      **PREP. TIME:** 10 min.      **COOK TIME:** 20 min.

## INGREDIENTS

- 4 salmon fillets
- ¼ cup soy sauce (low-sodium)
- 2 tablespoons honey
- 2 tablespoons rice vinegar
- 2 cloves garlic, minced
- 1 teaspoon ginger, minced
- 1 tablespoon sesame oil
- 1 tablespoon sesame seeds
- Green onions, chopped (for garnish)

## STEPS

1. In a bowl, mix soy sauce, honey, rice vinegar, garlic, ginger, and sesame oil.
2. Marinate salmon fillets in the mixture for at least 30 minutes.
3. Preheat oven to 375°F (190°C). Place salmon on a baking sheet.
4. Bake for 15-20 minutes until salmon is cooked through.

**NUTRITIONAL INFORMATIONS (PER SERVING):** 250 Calories, 25g. Proteins, 10g. Carbohydrates, 12g. Fats.

# Coconut Curry Chicken

SERVINGS: 4      PREP. TIME: 10 min.      COOK TIME: 20 min.

## INGREDIENTS

- 4 boneless, skinless chicken thighs
- 1 can (13.5 oz) coconut milk
- 2 tablespoons red curry paste
- 1 red bell pepper, sliced
- 1 yellow bell pepper, sliced
- 1 onion, sliced
- 2 cloves garlic, minced
- 1 tablespoon fresh ginger, minced
- 2 tablespoons olive oil
- Fresh cilantro, chopped (for garnish)
- Salt and pepper to taste

## STEPS

1. Heat olive oil in a large skillet over medium-high heat. Add garlic and ginger, and cook for 1 minute.
2. Add chicken thighs and cook for 5-7 minutes on each side until golden and cooked through. Remove from skillet and set aside.
3. In the same skillet, add onions, red bell pepper, and yellow bell pepper. Cook until tender.
4. Stir in coconut milk and red curry paste. Bring to a simmer.
5. Return chicken to the skillet and cook for an additional 5 minutes.
6. Season with salt and pepper, and garnish with fresh cilantro before serving.

**NUTRITIONAL INFORMATIONS (PER SERVING):** 380 Calories, 28g. Proteins, 8g. Carbohydrates, 22g. Fats.

# Pork Tenderloin with Apples & Onions

SERVINGS: 4      PREP. TIME: 10 min.      COOK TIME: 25 min.

## INGREDIENTS

- 1 pork tenderloin
- 2 apples, sliced
- 1 large onion, sliced
- 2 tablespoons olive oil
- ¼ cup apple cider vinegar
- 1 tablespoon fresh thyme, chopped
- Salt and pepper to taste

## STEPS

1. Preheat oven to 375°F (190°C).
2. Season pork tenderloin with salt and pepper.
3. In a large skillet, heat olive oil over medium-high heat. Brown the pork on all sides.
4. Transfer pork to a baking dish. In the same skillet, add apples, onions, apple cider vinegar, thyme, salt, and pepper. Cook for 5 minutes.
5. Pour apple and onion mixture over pork.
6. Bake for 20-25 minutes until pork is cooked through.

**NUTRITIONAL INFORMATIONS (PER SERVING):** 280 Calories, 28g. Proteins, 10g. Carbohydrates, 12g. Fats.

# Beef Fajita Bowls

**SERVINGS:** 4          **PREP. TIME:** 10 min.          **COOK TIME:** 15 min.

## INGREDIENTS

- 1 pound beef sirloin, sliced
- 1 red bell pepper, sliced
- 1 yellow bell pepper, sliced
- 1 green bell pepper, sliced
- 1 onion, sliced
- 2 tablespoons olive oil
- 1 tablespoon fajita seasoning
- 1 cup cauliflower rice
- ¼ cup fresh cilantro, chopped
- 1 lime, cut into wedges

## STEPS

1. Heat olive oil in a large skillet over medium-high heat. Add beef, fajita seasoning, and cook until browned, about 5-7 minutes.

2. Add bell peppers and onion, and cook for another 5-7 minutes until vegetables are tender.

3. Meanwhile, steam cauliflower rice until tender.

4. Serve beef and vegetable mixture over cauliflower rice, and garnish with fresh cilantro and lime wedges.

**NUTRITIONAL INFORMATIONS (PER SERVING):** 280 Calories, 25g. Proteins, 8g. Carbohydrates, 15g. Fats.

# Garlic Butter Steak Bites

**SERVINGS:** 4          **PREP. TIME:** 10 min.          **COOK TIME:** 10 min.

## INGREDIENTS

- 1 pound steak (sirloin or ribeye), cut into bite-sized pieces
- 4 tablespoons butter
- 4 cloves garlic, minced
- 1 tablespoon olive oil
- Salt and pepper to taste
- Fresh parsley, chopped (for garnish)

## STEPS

1. Heat olive oil in a large skillet over medium-high heat. Add steak pieces and season with salt and pepper.

2. Cook steak for 3-4 minutes until browned and cooked to desired doneness. Remove and set aside.

3. In the same skillet, add butter and garlic. Cook for 1-2 minutes until fragrant.

4. Return steak to the skillet and toss to coat with garlic butter.

5. Garnish with fresh parsley before serving.

**NUTRITIONAL INFORMATIONS (PER SERVING):** 320 Calories, 25g. Proteins, 2g. Carbohydrates, 20g. Fats.

# THAI COCONUT CHICKEN CURRY

**SERVINGS:** 4      **PREP. TIME:** 10 min.      **COOK TIME:** 20 min.

## INGREDIENTS

- 4 boneless, skinless chicken breasts, diced
- 1 can (13.5 oz) coconut milk
- 2 tablespoons red curry paste
- 1 red bell pepper, sliced
- 1 yellow bell pepper, sliced
- 1 onion, sliced
- 2 cloves garlic, minced
- 1 tablespoon fresh ginger, minced
- 2 tablespoons olive oil
- Fresh cilantro, chopped (for garnish)
- Salt and pepper to taste

## STEPS

1. Heat olive oil in a large skillet over medium-high heat. Add garlic and ginger, and cook for 1 minute.

2. Add chicken and cook until browned, about 5-7 minutes.

3. Add onions and bell peppers, and cook until tender.

4. Stir in coconut milk and red curry paste. Bring to a simmer.

5. Cook for an additional 5 minutes until chicken is cooked through.

6. Season with salt and pepper, and garnish with fresh cilantro before serving.

**NUTRITIONAL INFORMATIONS (PER SERVING):** 330 Calories, 28g. Proteins, 8g. Carbohydrates, 20g. Fats.

# LEMON DILL BAKED COD

**SERVINGS:** 4      **PREP. TIME:** 10 min.      **COOK TIME:** 20 min.

## INGREDIENTS

- 4 cod fillets
- 2 tablespoons olive oil
- 1 lemon, sliced
- 2 tablespoons fresh dill, chopped
- 2 cloves garlic, minced
- Salt and pepper to taste

## STEPS

1. Preheat oven to 375°F (190°C).

2. Place cod fillets on a baking sheet lined with parchment paper.

3. Drizzle with olive oil and top with lemon slices, dill, garlic, salt, and pepper.

4. Bake for 15-20 minutes until cod is opaque and flakes easily with a fork.

**NUTRITIONAL INFORMATIONS (PER SERVING):** 220 Calories, 25g. Proteins, 4g. Carbohydrates, 12g. Fats.

# Keto Chicken Alfredo Casserole

**SERVINGS:** 4     **PREP. TIME:** 10 min.     **COOK TIME:** 25 min.

## INGREDIENTS

- 4 boneless, skinless chicken breasts, cooked and shredded
- 1 cup heavy cream
- 1 cup grated Parmesan cheese
- ½ cup shredded mozzarella cheese
- ¼ cup cream cheese
- 2 cups broccoli florets, steamed
- 2 cloves garlic, minced
- Salt and pepper to taste

## STEPS

1. Preheat oven to 375°F (190°C).
2. In a saucepan over medium heat, combine heavy cream, Parmesan cheese, mozzarella cheese, cream cheese, and garlic. Cook, stirring constantly, until cheeses are melted and the sauce is smooth.
3. In a large bowl, combine shredded chicken, steamed broccoli, and the Alfredo sauce. Mix well.
4. Transfer the mixture to a baking dish and spread evenly.
5. Bake for 20-25 minutes until the casserole is bubbly and golden on top.

**NUTRITIONAL INFORMATIONS (PER SERVING):** 350 Calories, 30g. Proteins, 6g. Carbohydrates, 25g. Fats.

# Pesto Shrimp Zoodles

**SERVINGS:** 4     **PREP. TIME:** 10 min.     **COOK TIME:** 10 min.

## INGREDIENTS

- 1 pound shrimp, peeled and deveined
- 4 zucchinis, spiralized
- ½ cup pesto sauce
- ¼ cup cherry tomatoes, halved
- ¼ cup grated Parmesan cheese
- 2 tablespoons olive oil
- Salt and pepper to taste

## STEPS

1. Heat olive oil in a large skillet over medium heat. Add shrimp and cook until pink, about 3-4 minutes.
2. Add zucchini noodles and cook for 2-3 minutes until tender.
3. Stir in pesto sauce and cherry tomatoes, and cook for another 2 minutes.
4. Serve topped with grated Parmesan cheese.

**NUTRITIONAL INFORMATIONS (PER SERVING):** 280 Calories, 25g. Proteins, 6g. Carbohydrates, 18g. Fats.

# DESSERTS

# COCONUT LIME PROTEIN BALLS

**SERVINGS:** 4      **PREP. TIME:** 10 min.      **COOK TIME:** none

## INGREDIENTS

- 1 cup almond flour
- ½ cup vanilla protein powder
- ¼ cup unsweetened shredded coconut
- ¼ cup coconut oil, melted
- 2 tablespoons stevia or erythritol
- Zest of 1 lime
- 1 tablespoon lime juice

## STEPS

1. In a bowl, mix almond flour, protein powder, shredded coconut, melted coconut oil, stevia, lime zest, and lime juice until well combined.

2. Roll mixture into small balls and *refrigerate for at least 30 minutes* before serving.

**NUTRITIONAL INFORMATIONS (PER SERVING):** 180 Calories, 12g. Proteins, 6g. Carbohydrates, 15g. Fats.

# COCONUT ALMOND PROTEIN BITES

**SERVINGS:** 4      **PREP. TIME:** 10 min.      **COOK TIME:** none

## INGREDIENTS

- 1 cup almond flour
- ½ cup vanilla protein powder
- ¼ cup unsweetened shredded coconut
- ¼ cup almond butter
- 2 tablespoons stevia or erythritol
- 1 teaspoon vanilla extract

## STEPS

1. In a bowl, mix almond flour, protein powder, shredded coconut, almond butter, stevia, and vanilla extract until well combined.

2. Roll mixture into small balls and *refrigerate for at least 30 minutes* before serving.

**NUTRITIONAL INFORMATIONS (PER SERVING):** 180 Calories, 15g. Proteins, 5g. Carbohydrates, 15g. Fats.

# CHOCOLATE PROTEIN PUDDING

**SERVINGS:** 4 | **PREP. TIME:** 10 min. | **COOK TIME:** none

## INGREDIENTS

- 2 cups unsweetened almond milk
- ½ cup chocolate protein powder
- ¼ cup unsweetened cocoa powder
- ¼ cup chia seeds
- 2 tablespoons stevia or erythritol
- 1 teaspoon vanilla extract

## STEPS

1. In a bowl, whisk together almond milk, protein powder, cocoa powder, chia seeds, stevia, and vanilla extract until smooth.

2. ***Refrigerate for at least 2 hours or overnight*** until thickened.

3. Serve chilled.

**NUTRITIONAL INFORMATIONS (PER SERVING):** 180 Calories, 15g. Proteins, 6g. Carbohydrates, 10g. Fats.

# LEMON RASPBERRY PROTEIN BARS

**SERVINGS:** 4 | **PREP. TIME:** 10 min. | **COOK TIME:** none

## INGREDIENTS

- 1 cup almond flour
- ½ cup vanilla protein powder
- ¼ cup stevia or erythritol
- ¼ cup coconut oil, melted
- 2 tablespoons lemon juice
- 1 tablespoon lemon zest
- ½ cup fresh raspberries

## STEPS

1. In a bowl, mix almond flour, protein powder, stevia, melted coconut oil, lemon juice, and lemon zest until well combined.

2. Gently fold in fresh raspberries.

3. Press mixture into a lined baking dish.

4. ***Refrigerate for at least 1 hour*** until firm.

5. Cut into bars and serve.

**NUTRITIONAL INFORMATIONS (PER SERVING):** 180 Calories, 12g. Proteins, 8g. Carbohydrates, 15g. Fats.

# PUMPKIN PROTEIN MUFFINS

**SERVINGS:** 4      **PREP. TIME:** 10 min.      **COOK TIME:** 25 min.

## INGREDIENTS

- 1 cup almond flour
- ½ cup vanilla protein powder
- ½ cup pumpkin puree
- ¼ cup stevia or erythritol
- 2 large eggs
- ¼ cup coconut oil, melted
- 1 teaspoon baking powder
- 1 teaspoon pumpkin spice
- 1 teaspoon vanilla extract

## STEPS

1. Preheat oven to 350°F (175°C). Line a muffin tin with paper liners.

2. In a bowl, mix almond flour, protein powder, baking powder, pumpkin spice, and stevia.

3. In another bowl, whisk pumpkin puree, eggs, coconut oil, and vanilla extract.

4. Combine wet and dry ingredients.

5. Spoon batter into muffin tin and bake for 20-25 minutes until a toothpick inserted comes out clean.

**NUTRITIONAL INFORMATIONS (PER SERVING):** 220 Calories, 15g. Proteins, 8g. Carbohydrates, 15g. Fats.

# STRAWBERRY PROTEIN CHEESECAKE

**SERVINGS:** 4      **PREP. TIME:** 10 min.      **COOK TIME:** none

## INGREDIENTS

- 1 cup Greek yogurt (full-fat, unsweetened)
- ½ cup strawberry protein powder
- ¼ cup cream cheese, softened
- 2 tablespoons stevia or erythritol
- 1 teaspoon vanilla extract
- ½ cup fresh strawberries, sliced

## STEPS

1. In a bowl, mix Greek yogurt, protein powder, cream cheese, stevia, and vanilla extract until smooth.

2. Pour mixture into serving dishes and top with sliced strawberries.

3. ***Refrigerate for at least 1 hour*** before serving.

**NUTRITIONAL INFORMATIONS (PER SERVING):** 180 Calories, 20g. Proteins, 8g. Carbohydrates, 8g. Fats.

# PEANUT BUTTER COOKIES

**SERVINGS:** 4      **PREP. TIME:** 10 min.      **COOK TIME:** 12 min.

## INGREDIENTS

- 1 cup natural peanut butter
- ½ cup stevia or erythritol
- 1 large egg
- 1 teaspoon vanilla extract
- Pinch of salt

## STEPS

1. Preheat oven to 350°F (175°C).
2. In a bowl, mix peanut butter, stevia, egg, vanilla extract, and salt until well combined.
3. Roll the dough into small balls and place on a baking sheet lined with parchment paper.
4. Flatten each ball with a fork.
5. Bake for 10-12 minutes until golden brown.

**NUTRITIONAL INFORMATIONS (PER SERVING):** 180 Calories, 6g. Proteins, 5g. Carbohydrates, 15g. Fats.

# MOCHA MOUSSE

**SERVINGS:** 4      **PREP. TIME:** 10 min.      **COOK TIME:** none

## INGREDIENTS

- 1 cup Greek yogurt (full-fat, unsweetened)
- ½ cup chocolate protein powder
- 2 tablespoons unsweetened cocoa powder
- 1 tablespoon instant coffee granules
- 2 tablespoons stevia or erythritol
- 1 teaspoon vanilla extract

## STEPS

1. In a bowl, mix Greek yogurt, protein powder, cocoa powder, coffee granules, stevia, and vanilla extract until smooth.
2. Spoon into serving dishes and ***chill for at least 30 minutes*** before serving.

**NUTRITIONAL INFORMATIONS (PER SERVING):** 170 Calories, 20g. Proteins, 6g. Carbohydrates, 8g. Fats.

# CHOCOLATE CHIP COOKIES

**SERVINGS:** 4      **PREP. TIME:** 10 min.      **COOK TIME:** 12 min.

## INGREDIENTS

- 1 cup almond flour
- ½ cup vanilla protein powder
- ¼ cup butter, softened
- ¼ cup stevia or erythritol
- 1 large egg
- 1 teaspoon vanilla extract
- ½ cup sugar-free chocolate chips

## STEPS

1. Preheat oven to 350°F (175°C). Line a baking sheet with parchment paper.
2. In a bowl, mix almond flour, protein powder, and stevia.
3. In another bowl, beat butter, egg, and vanilla extract until smooth.
4. Combine wet and dry ingredients and fold in chocolate chips.
5. Drop spoonfuls of dough onto the baking sheet.
6. Bake for 10-12 minutes until golden brown.

**NUTRITIONAL INFORMATIONS (PER SERVING):** 230 Calories, 15g. Proteins, 8g. Carbohydrates, 18g. Fats.

# MATCHA LATTE

**SERVINGS:** 4      **PREP. TIME:** 5 min.      **COOK TIME:** none

## INGREDIENTS

- 2 cups unsweetened almond milk
- ½ cup vanilla protein powder
- 2 tablespoons matcha green tea powder
- 2 tablespoons stevia or erythritol
- 1 teaspoon vanilla extract

## STEPS

1. In a blender, combine almond milk, protein powder, matcha powder, stevia, and vanilla extract. Blend until smooth.
2. Serve immediately.

**NUTRITIONAL INFORMATIONS (PER SERVING):** 100 Calories, 12g. Proteins, 6g. Carbohydrates, 6g. Fats.

# COCONUT PROTEIN TRUFFLES

**SERVINGS:** 4                    **PREP. TIME:** 10 min.                    **COOK TIME:** none

## INGREDIENTS

- 1 cup unsweetened shredded coconut

- ½ cup vanilla protein powder

- ¼ cup coconut oil, melted

- 2 tablespoons stevia or erythritol

- 1 teaspoon vanilla extract

## STEPS

1. In a bowl, mix shredded coconut, protein powder, melted coconut oil, stevia, and vanilla extract until well combined.

2. Roll mixture into small balls and ***refrigerate for at least 30 minutes*** before serving.

**NUTRITIONAL INFORMATIONS (PER SERVING):** 180 Calories, 12g. Proteins, 5g. Carbohydrates, 15g. Fats.

# APPLE CINNAMON MUFFINS

**SERVINGS:** 4                    **PREP. TIME:** 10 min.                    **COOK TIME:** 25 min.

## INGREDIENTS

- 1 cup almond flour
- ½ cup vanilla protein powder
- ½ cup unsweetened applesauce
- ¼ cup stevia or erythritol
- 2 large eggs
- ¼ cup coconut oil, melted
- 1 teaspoon baking powder
- 1 teaspoon ground cinnamon
- 1 teaspoon vanilla extract

## STEPS

1. Preheat oven to 350°F (175°C). Line a muffin tin with paper liners.

2. In a bowl, mix almond flour, protein powder, baking powder, cinnamon, and stevia.

3. In another bowl, whisk applesauce, eggs, coconut oil, and vanilla extract.

4. Combine wet and dry ingredients.

5. Spoon batter into muffin tin and bake for 20-25 minutes until a toothpick inserted comes out clean.

**NUTRITIONAL INFORMATIONS (PER SERVING):** 220 Calories, 15g. Proteins, 10g. Carbohydrates, 15g. Fats.

# CHOCOLATE MINT PROTEIN BARS

**SERVINGS:** 4      **PREP. TIME:** 10 min.      **COOK TIME:** none

## INGREDIENTS

- 1 cup almond flour

- ½ cup chocolate protein powder

- ¼ cup unsweetened cocoa powder

- ¼ cup stevia or erythritol

- ¼ cup coconut oil, melted

- ½ teaspoon mint extract

## STEPS

1. In a bowl, mix almond flour, protein powder, cocoa powder, stevia, melted coconut oil, and mint extract until well combined.

2. Press mixture into a lined baking dish.

3. ***Refrigerate for at least 1 hour*** until firm.

4. Cut into bars and serve.

**NUTRITIONAL INFORMATIONS (PER SERVING):** 220 Calories, 12g. Proteins, 6g. Carbohydrates, 18g. Fats.

# VANILLA ICE CREAM

**SERVINGS:** 4      **PREP. TIME:** 10 min.      **COOK TIME:** none

## INGREDIENTS

- 1 cup unsweetened almond milk

- ½ cup heavy cream

- ½ cup vanilla protein powder

- ¼ cup stevia or erythritol

- 1 teaspoon vanilla extract

## STEPS

1. In a blender, blend almond milk, heavy cream, protein powder, stevia, and vanilla extract until smooth.

2. Pour mixture into an ice cream maker and churn according to the manufacturer's instructions.

3. Serve immediately or freeze for a firmer texture.

**NUTRITIONAL INFORMATIONS (PER SERVING):** 180 Calories, 10g. Proteins, 4g. Carbohydrates, 15g. Fats.

# Vanilla Almond Protein Balls

**SERVINGS:** 4      **PREP. TIME:** 10 min.      **COOK TIME:** none

## INGREDIENTS

- 1 cup almond flour

- ¼ cup vanilla protein powder

- ¼ cup almond butter

- 2 tablespoons stevia or erythritol

- 1 teaspoon vanilla extract

- 2 tablespoons unsweetened almond milk

## STEPS

1. In a bowl, mix almond flour, protein powder, almond butter, stevia, and vanilla extract.

2. Add almond milk and mix until a dough forms.

3. Roll into small balls and ***refrigerate for at least 30 minutes*** before serving.

**NUTRITIONAL INFORMATIONS (PER SERVING):** 160 Calories, 8g. Proteins, 5g. Carbohydrates, 12g. Fats.

# Berry Gelatin

**SERVINGS:** 4      **PREP. TIME:** 10 min.      **COOK TIME:** none

## INGREDIENTS

- 2 cups water

- 1 cup mixed berries (strawberries, blueberries, raspberries)

- ¼ cup stevia or erythritol

- 1 tablespoon gelatin

- ½ cup vanilla protein powder

## STEPS

1. In a saucepan, heat water and stevia until hot (do not boil).

2. Stir in gelatin until dissolved.

3. Remove from heat and let cool slightly.

4. Blend mixed berries and protein powder in a blender until smooth.

5. Mix berry blend with gelatin mixture and pour into serving dishes.

6. ***Refrigerate for at least 2 hours*** until set.

**NUTRITIONAL INFORMATIONS (PER SERVING):** 70 Calories, 12g. Proteins, 6g. Carbohydrates, 1g. Fats.

# PEANUT BUTTER CUPS

**SERVINGS:** 4     **PREP. TIME:** 10 min.     **COOK TIME:** none

## INGREDIENTS

- ½ cup natural peanut butter
- ¼ cup coconut oil, melted
- ¼ cup chocolate protein powder
- 2 tablespoons stevia or erythritol
- ¼ cup dark chocolate chips (85% cocoa or higher)

## STEPS

1. In a bowl, mix peanut butter, melted coconut oil, protein powder, and stevia until smooth.
2. Pour mixture into silicone cupcake molds.
3. Top with a few dark chocolate chips.
4. ***Freeze for at least 1 hour*** until solid.

**NUTRITIONAL INFORMATIONS (PER SERVING):** 210 Calories, 12g. Proteins, 6g. Carbohydrates, 20g. Fats.

# CINNAMON ROLL BITES

**SERVINGS:** 4     **PREP. TIME:** 10 min.     **COOK TIME:** 20 min.

## INGREDIENTS

- 1 cup almond flour
- ½ cup vanilla protein powder
- ¼ cup coconut flour
- ¼ cup stevia or erythritol
- 1 teaspoon ground cinnamon
- ¼ cup coconut oil, melted
- 2 large eggs
- 1 teaspoon vanilla extract

## STEPS

1. Preheat oven to 350°F (175°C). Line a baking sheet with parchment paper.
2. In a bowl, mix almond flour, protein powder, coconut flour, stevia, and ground cinnamon.
3. In another bowl, whisk melted coconut oil, eggs, and vanilla extract.
4. Combine wet and dry ingredients.
5. Roll mixture into small balls and place on the baking sheet.
6. Bake for 15-20 minutes until golden brown.

**NUTRITIONAL INFORMATIONS (PER SERVING):** 180 Calories, 15g. Proteins, 6g. Carbohydrates, 15g. Fats.

# CHOCOLATE BANANA BREAD

**SERVINGS:** 4      **PREP. TIME:** 10 min.      **COOK TIME:** 40 min.

## INGREDIENTS

- 1 cup almond flour
- ½ cup chocolate protein powder
- ¼ cup coconut flour
- ¼ cup stevia or erythritol
- ½ cup mashed ripe bananas
- 2 large eggs
- ¼ cup coconut oil, melted
- 1 teaspoon baking powder
- 1 teaspoon vanilla extract
- ½ teaspoon ground cinnamon

## STEPS

1. Preheat oven to 350°F (175°C). Grease a loaf pan.

2. In a bowl, mix almond flour, protein powder, coconut flour, baking powder, cinnamon, and stevia.

3. In another bowl, whisk mashed bananas, eggs, coconut oil, and vanilla extract.

4. Combine wet and dry ingredients.

5. Pour batter into loaf pan and bake for 35-40 minutes until a toothpick inserted comes out clean.

**NUTRITIONAL INFORMATIONS (PER SERVING):** 220 Calories, 15g. Proteins, 10g. Carbohydrates, 15g. Fats.

# CHOCOLATE COCONUT BARS

**SERVINGS:** 4      **PREP. TIME:** 10 min.      **COOK TIME:** none

## INGREDIENTS

- 1 cup unsweetened shredded coconut
- 1/2 cup chocolate protein powder
- 1/4 cup coconut oil, melted
- 2 tablespoons stevia or erythritol
- 1 teaspoon vanilla extract

## STEPS

1. In a bowl, mix shredded coconut, protein powder, melted coconut oil, stevia, and vanilla extract until well combined.

2. Press mixture into a lined baking dish.

3. ***Refrigerate for at least 1 hour*** until firm.

4. Cut into bars and serve.

**NUTRITIONAL INFORMATIONS (PER SERVING):** 220 Calories, 15g. Proteins, 6g. Carbohydrates, 20g. Fats.

# SMOOTHIES

# BERRY ALMOND SMOOTHIE

**SERVINGS:** 1      **PREP. TIME:** 5 min.      **COOK TIME:** none

## INGREDIENTS

- 1 cup unsweetened almond milk

- ½ cup Greek yogurt (full-fat, unsweetened)

- ½ cup mixed berries (strawberries, blueberries, raspberries)

- 1 scoop vanilla protein powder

- 1 tablespoon almond butter

- 1 teaspoon stevia or erythritol

## STEPS

1. Combine all ingredients in a blender.

2. Blend until smooth.

3. Serve immediately.

**NUTRITIONAL INFORMATIONS (PER SERVING):** 180 Calories, 20g. Proteins, 8g. Carbohydrates, 10g. Fats.


# PEANUT BUTTER BANANA SMOOTHIE

**SERVINGS:** 1      **PREP. TIME:** 5 min.      **COOK TIME:** none

## INGREDIENTS

- ½ banana

- 1 cup Greek yogurt (full-fat, unsweetened)

- 1 cup unsweetened almond milk

- 2 tablespoons natural peanut butter

- 1 teaspoon stevia or erythritol

## STEPS

1. Combine all ingredients in a blender.

2. Blend until smooth.

3. Serve immediately.

**NUTRITIONAL INFORMATIONS (PER SERVING):** 240 Calories, 18g. Proteins, 15g. Carbohydrates, 14g. Fats.

# GREEK YOGURT BERRY SMOOTHIE

**SERVINGS:** 1                    **PREP. TIME:** 5 min.                    **COOK TIME:** none

## INGREDIENTS

- 1 cup Greek yogurt (full-fat, unsweetened)

- ½ cup mixed berries (strawberries, blueberries, raspberries)

- ½ cup unsweetened almond milk

- 1 tablespoon chia seeds

- 1 teaspoon stevia or erythritol

## STEPS

1. Combine all ingredients in a blender.

2. Blend until smooth.

3. Serve immediately.

**NUTRITIONAL INFORMATIONS (PER SERVING):** 180 Calories, 20g. Proteins, 10g. Carbohydrates, 8g. Fats.

# GREEN PROTEIN SMOOTHIE

**SERVINGS:** 1                    **PREP. TIME:** 5 min.                    **COOK TIME:** none

## INGREDIENTS

- 1 cup spinach

- ½ cup unsweetened almond milk

- ½ cup Greek yogurt (full-fat, unsweetened)

- ½ avocado

- 1 scoop vanilla protein powder

- 1 tablespoon chia seeds

- 1 teaspoon stevia or erythritol

## STEPS

1. Combine all ingredients in a blender.

2. Blend until smooth.

3. Serve immediately.

**NUTRITIONAL INFORMATIONS (PER SERVING):** 200 Calories, 18g. Proteins, 7g. Carbohydrates, 15g. Fats.

# CHOCOLATE BANANA SMOOTHIE

| SERVINGS: 1 | PREP. TIME: 5 min. | COOK TIME: none |
|---|---|---|

## INGREDIENTS

- 1 cup unsweetened almond milk

- ½ banana

- 1 scoop chocolate protein powder

- 1 tablespoon peanut butter

- 1 teaspoon unsweetened cocoa powder

## STEPS

1. Combine all ingredients in a blender.

2. Blend until smooth.

3. Serve immediately.

**NUTRITIONAL INFORMATIONS (PER SERVING):** 220 Calories, 22g. Proteins, 12g. Carbohydrates, 12g. Fats.

# COCONUT MANGO SMOOTHIE

| SERVINGS: 1 | PREP. TIME: 5 min. | COOK TIME: none |
|---|---|---|

## INGREDIENTS

- 1 cup coconut milk

- ½ cup frozen mango chunks

- ½ cup Greek yogurt (full-fat, unsweetened)

- 1 tablespoon unsweetened shredded coconut

- 1 teaspoon stevia or erythritol

## STEPS

1. Combine all ingredients in a blender.

2. Blend until smooth.

3. Serve immediately.

**NUTRITIONAL INFORMATIONS (PER SERVING):** 220 Calories, 14g. Proteins, 12g. Carbohydrates, 15g. Fats.

# BROCCOLI APPLE SMOOTHIE

**SERVINGS:** 1　　　　**PREP. TIME:** 5 min.　　　　**COOK TIME:** none

## INGREDIENTS

- 4 cups broccoli, chopped

- 2 apples, chopped

- 4 cups unsweetened almond milk

- 2 cups Greek yogurt (full-fat, unsweetened)

- 4 tablespoons chia seeds

- 4 teaspoons stevia or erythritol

## STEPS

1. Combine all ingredients in a blender.

2. Blend until smooth.

3. Serve immediately.

**NUTRITIONAL INFORMATIONS (PER SERVING):** 190 Calories, 17g. Proteins, 12g. Carbohydrates, 8g. Fats.

# VANILLA BLUEBERRY SMOOTHIE

**SERVINGS:** 1　　　　**PREP. TIME:** 5 min.　　　　**COOK TIME:** none

## INGREDIENTS

- 1 cup unsweetened almond milk

- ½ cup Greek yogurt (full-fat, unsweetened)

- ½ cup fresh blueberries

- 1 scoop vanilla protein powder

- 1 teaspoon vanilla extract

## STEPS

1. Combine all ingredients in a blender.

2. Blend until smooth.

3. Serve immediately.

**NUTRITIONAL INFORMATIONS (PER SERVING):** 180 Calories, 20g. Proteins, 10g. Carbohydrates, 8g. Fats.

# PEANUT BUTTER CUP SMOOTHIE

SERVINGS: 1                PREP. TIME: 5 min.                COOK TIME: none

## INGREDIENTS

- 1 cup unsweetened almond milk
- 1 scoop chocolate protein powder
- 2 tablespoons natural peanut butter
- 1 teaspoon stevia or erythritol

## STEPS

1. Combine all ingredients in a blender.
2. Blend until smooth.
3. Serve immediately.

**NUTRITIONAL INFORMATIONS (PER SERVING):** 240 Calories, 24g. Proteins, 6g. Carbohydrates, 18g. Fats.

# BLUEBERRY ALMOND SMOOTHIE

SERVINGS: 1                PREP. TIME: 5 min.                COOK TIME: none

## INGREDIENTS

- ½ cup fresh blueberries
- 1 cup Greek yogurt (full-fat, unsweetened)
- 1 cup unsweetened almond milk
- 1 tablespoon almond butter
- 1 teaspoon vanilla extract
- 1 teaspoon stevia or erythritol

## STEPS

1. Combine all ingredients in a blender.
2. Blend until smooth.
3. Serve immediately.

**NUTRITIONAL INFORMATIONS (PER SERVING):** 200 Calories, 18g. Proteins, 10g. Carbohydrates, 12g. Fats.

# CHOCOLATE HAZELNUT SMOOTHIE

**SERVINGS:** 1      **PREP. TIME:** 5 min.      **COOK TIME:** none

## INGREDIENTS

- 1 cup Greek yogurt (full-fat, unsweetened)
- 1 cup unsweetened almond milk
- 1 tablespoon unsweetened cocoa powder
- 2 tablespoons hazelnut butter
- 1 teaspoon stevia or erythritol

## STEPS

1. Combine all ingredients in a blender.
2. Blend until smooth.
3. Serve immediately.

**NUTRITIONAL INFORMATIONS (PER SERVING):** 210 Calories, 16g. Proteins, 8g. Carbohydrates, 14g. Fats.

# CHOCOLATE CHERRY SMOOTHIE

**SERVINGS:** 1      **PREP. TIME:** 5 min.      **COOK TIME:** none

## INGREDIENTS

- 1 cup unsweetened almond milk
- ½ cup frozen cherries
- 1 scoop chocolate protein powder
- 1 tablespoon unsweetened cocoa powder
- 1 teaspoon stevia or erythritol

## STEPS

1. Combine all ingredients in a blender.
2. Blend until smooth.
3. Serve immediately.

**NUTRITIONAL INFORMATIONS (PER SERVING):** 200 Calories, 20g. Proteins, 12g. Carbohydrates, 8g. Fats.

# CARROT GINGER SMOOTHIE

**SERVINGS:** 1         **PREP. TIME:** 5 min.         **COOK TIME:** none

## INGREDIENTS

- 4 cups carrots, chopped
- 2 inches fresh ginger, peeled and chopped
- 4 cups unsweetened almond milk
- 2 cups Greek yogurt (full-fat, unsweetened)
- 4 tablespoons chia seeds
- 4 teaspoons stevia or erythritol

## STEPS

1. Combine all ingredients in a blender.
2. Blend until smooth.
3. Serve immediately.

**NUTRITIONAL INFORMATIONS (PER SERVING):** 180 Calories, 16g. Proteins, 12g. Carbohydrates, 8g. Fats.

# PUMPKIN SPICE SMOOTHIE

**SERVINGS:** 1         **PREP. TIME:** 5 min.         **COOK TIME:** none

## INGREDIENTS

- 1 cup pumpkin puree
- 1 cup Greek yogurt (full-fat, unsweetened)
- 1 cup unsweetened almond milk
- 1 tablespoon chia seeds
- 1 teaspoon pumpkin spice
- 1 teaspoon stevia or erythritol

## STEPS

1. Combine all ingredients in a blender.
2. Blend until smooth.
3. Serve immediately.

**NUTRITIONAL INFORMATIONS (PER SERVING):** 180 Calories, 18g. Proteins, 8g. Carbohydrates, 10g. Fats.

# Strawberry Avocado Smoothie

**SERVINGS:** 1                     **PREP. TIME:** 5 min.                     **COOK TIME:** none

## INGREDIENTS

- ½ avocado

- 1 cup fresh strawberries

- 1 cup Greek yogurt (full-fat, unsweetened)

- 1 cup unsweetened almond milk

- 1 teaspoon vanilla extract

- 1 teaspoon stevia or erythritol

## STEPS

1. Combine all ingredients in a blender.

2. Blend until smooth.

3. Serve immediately.

**NUTRITIONAL INFORMATIONS (PER SERVING):** 220 Calories, 15g. Proteins, 9g. Carbohydrates, 15g. Fats.

# Mocha Protein Smoothie

**SERVINGS:** 1                     **PREP. TIME:** 5 min.                     **COOK TIME:** none

## INGREDIENTS

- 1 cup unsweetened almond milk

- 1 scoop chocolate protein powder

- 1 tablespoon instant coffee granules

- 1 tablespoon unsweetened cocoa powder

- 1 teaspoon stevia or erythritol

## STEPS

1. Combine all ingredients in a blender.

2. Blend until smooth.

3. Serve immediately.

**NUTRITIONAL INFORMATIONS (PER SERVING):** 180 Calories, 22g. Proteins, 6g. Carbohydrates, 10g. Fats.

# LEMON BLUEBERRY SMOOTHIE

**SERVINGS:** 1      **PREP. TIME:** 5 min.      **COOK TIME:** none

## INGREDIENTS

- ½ cup fresh blueberries

- 1 cup Greek yogurt (full-fat, unsweetened)

- 1 cup unsweetened almond milk

- 1 tablespoon chia seeds

- Zest and juice of 1 lemon

- 1 teaspoon stevia or erythritol

## STEPS

1. Combine all ingredients in a blender.

2. Blend until smooth.

3. Serve immediately.

**NUTRITIONAL INFORMATIONS (PER SERVING):** 190 Calories, 18g. Proteins, 9g. Carbohydrates, 10g. Fats.

# TOMATO BASIL SMOOTHIE

**SERVINGS:** 1      **PREP. TIME:** 5 min.      **COOK TIME:** none

## INGREDIENTS

- 4 cups tomatoes, chopped

- ¼ cup fresh basil leaves

- 4 cups unsweetened almond milk

- 2 cups Greek yogurt (full-fat, unsweetened)

- 4 tablespoons chia seeds

- 4 teaspoons stevia or erythritol

## STEPS

1. Combine all ingredients in a blender.

2. Blend until smooth.

3. Serve immediately.

**NUTRITIONAL INFORMATIONS (PER SERVING):** 170 Calories, 15g. Proteins, 7g. Carbohydrates, 8g. Fats.

# MINT CHOCOLATE SMOOTHIE

**SERVINGS:** 1      **PREP. TIME:** 5 min.      **COOK TIME:** none

## INGREDIENTS

- 1 cup unsweetened almond milk
- 1 scoop chocolate protein powder
- ¼ teaspoon mint extract
- 1 tablespoon unsweetened cocoa powder
- 1 teaspoon stevia or erythritol

## STEPS

1. Combine all ingredients in a blender.
2. Blend until smooth.
3. Serve immediately.

**NUTRITIONAL INFORMATIONS (PER SERVING):** 180 Calories, 22g. Proteins, 5g. Carbohydrates, 10g. Fats.

# RASPBERRY COCONUT SMOOTHIE

**SERVINGS:** 1      **PREP. TIME:** 5 min.      **COOK TIME:** none

## INGREDIENTS

- ½ cup fresh raspberries
- 1 cup coconut milk
- 1 cup Greek yogurt (full-fat, unsweetened)
- 1 tablespoon unsweetened shredded coconut
- 1 teaspoon stevia or erythritol

## STEPS

1. Combine all ingredients in a blender.
2. Blend until smooth.
3. Serve immediately.

**NUTRITIONAL INFORMATIONS (PER SERVING):** 200 Calories, 16g. Proteins, 8g. Carbohydrates, 12g. Fats.

# MEAL PLAN

# How to Use This Meal Plan for Optimal Results

Welcome to the 60-Day Low-Carb, High-Protein Meal Plan! This plan is designed to help you lose weight and build muscle through carefully balanced meals that are low in carbohydrates and high in protein. Here are some tips and tricks to maximize your success:

**Consistency is Key**: Stick to the meal plan as closely as possible. Consistency in your diet will help you see the best results.

**Portion Control**: Pay attention to portion sizes. Eating the correct portions will ensure you're not consuming too many calories, which is crucial for weight loss.

**Hydration**: Drink plenty of water throughout the day. Staying hydrated is essential for muscle function and overall health.

**Exercise Regularly**: Incorporate both cardio and strength training exercises into your routine. Exercise will help you burn calories and build muscle more effectively.

**Meal Prep**: Plan and prepare your meals in advance. This will help you stick to the meal plan and avoid unhealthy choices.

**Listen to Your Body**: Everyone's body is different. Pay attention to how your body responds to the meal plan and adjust as necessary.

**Get Enough Sleep**: Ensure you are getting at least 7-8 hours of sleep per night. Adequate sleep is crucial for muscle recovery and overall well-being.

**Mindful Eating**: Eat slowly and savor your meals. This will help you feel more satisfied and prevent overeating.

By following these guidelines and the meal plan provided, you can achieve your weight loss and muscle-building goals. Remember, the journey is just as important as the destination, so enjoy the process and celebrate your progress along the way!

# Daily Caloric and Nutrient Needs

*For an average adult aiming to lose weight and build muscle, daily nutritional requirements are approximately:*

*Calories*: 1,500-2,000

*Protein*: 100-150 grams

*Carbohydrates*: 50-150 grams

*Fat*: 50-70 grams

These values can vary based on individual factors such as age, gender, activity level, and metabolic rate. The meal plan below is structured to meet these requirements, with a focus on nutrient-dense foods.

# 60-DAY MEAL PLAN

This meal plan is designed for those who enjoy tasting a variety of delicious dishes every day. The plan is carefully structured with detailed nutritional information, including calorie counts, allowing you to freely modify it based on your preferences and dietary needs.

## Flexibility and Personalization

One of the key features of this meal plan is its flexibility. While we have provided a different dish for each day to keep things exciting and varied, you can easily repeat meals on consecutive days if you find certain recipes particularly enjoyable. The structure of the plan makes it simple to replace one meal with another by keeping the calorie count in mind.

For instance, if you enjoy a particular lunch recipe, feel free to have it multiple times a week. Just ensure that the total calorie intake remains consistent with the guidelines provided for each day.

## Modifying the Meal Plan

To make modifications:

*Identify the Caloric Value*: Look at the calories indicated for the meal you wish to replace.

*Choose a Substitute*: Select another recipe from the plan or your favorite meal that has a similar caloric value.

*Balance Your Day*: Ensure that the overall daily intake aligns with your calorie goals to maintain a balanced diet.

## Snack and Dessert Flexibility

The snack or dessert in this meal plan can be incorporated into one of the three main meals or enjoyed as a mid-morning or mid-afternoon snack.

You can also replace the snack or dessert with something else that matches the caloric content, such as a smoothie, another dessert, or a different type of snack. Smoothies are a great way to add extra calories while keeping your meals nutritious and balanced. You can easily include it as an additional snack during the day or incorporate it into one of your three main meals.

By following this flexible and personalized approach, you can enjoy a diverse range of meals while effectively working towards your weight loss and muscle-building goals. Enjoy your culinary journey and the path to a healthier you!

## WEEK 1

| DAY 1 | | | |
|---|---|---|---|
| **BREAKFAST** | Greek Yogurt Parfait with Berries & Nuts | 220 Cal. | (p. 16) |
| **LUNCH** | Grilled Chicken Caesar Salad | 320 Cal. | (p. 28) |
| **DINNER** | Grilled Steak with Chimichurri Sauce | 370 Cal. | (p. 40) |
| **SNACK / DESSERT** | Coconut Lime Protein Balls | 180 Cal. | (p. 52) |
| DAY 2 | | | |
| **BREAKFAST** | Spinach & Feta Omelette | 220 Cal. | (p. 16) |
| **LUNCH** | Turkey Avocado Wrap | 280 Cal. | (p. 28) |
| **DINNER** | Baked Lemon Herb Salmon | 290 Cal. | (p. 40) |
| **SNACK / DESSERT** | Chocolate Protein Pudding | 180 Cal. | (p. 53) |
| DAY 3 | | | |
| **BREAKFAST** | Avocado & Smoked Salmon Toast | 300 Cal. | (p. 17) |
| **LUNCH** | Baked Salmon with Dill & Lemon | 290 Cal. | (p. 29) |
| **DINNER** | Balsamic Glazed Chicken | 280 Cal. | (p. 41) |
| **SNACK / DESSERT** | Coconut Almond Protein Bites | 180 Cal. | (p. 52) |

| DAY 4 | | | |
|---|---|---|---|
| BREAKFAST | Scrambled Eggs with Spinach & Tomatoes | 230 Cal. | (p. 18) |
| LUNCH | Egg Plant Lasagna | 380 Cal. | (p. 29) |
| DINNER | Lemon Garlic Shrimp Pasta | 280 Cal. | (p. 41) |
| SNACK / DESSERT | Lemon Raspberry Protein Bars | 180 Cal. | (p. 53) |

| DAY 5 | | | |
|---|---|---|---|
| BREAKFAST | Egg Muffins | 120 Cal. | (p. 19) |
| LUNCH | Shrimp & Avocado Salad | 280 Cal. | (p. 30) |
| DINNER | Spicy Turkey & Zucchini Skillet | 400 Cal. | (p. 42) |
| SNACK / DESSERT | Pumpkin Protein Muffins | 220 Cal. | (p. 54) |

| DAY 6 | | | |
|---|---|---|---|
| BREAKFAST | Chia Seed Pudding with Almond Milk & Berries | 180 Cal. | (p. 18) |
| LUNCH | Grilled Chicken & Pesto Wrap | 350 Cal. | (p. 30) |
| DINNER | Garlic Butter Shrimp with Asparagus | 280 Cal. | (p. 42) |
| SNACK / DESSERT | Strawberry Protein Cheesecake | 180 Cal. | (p. 54) |

| DAY 7 | | | |
|---|---|---|---|
| BREAKFAST | Oats with Almond Butter & Bananas | 250 Cal. | (p. 19) |
| LUNCH | Chicken & Vegetable Skewers | 250 Cal. | (p. 31) |
| DINNER | Lamb Chops with Mint Yogurt Sauce | 340 Cal. | (p. 43) |
| SNACK / DESSERT | Peanut Butter Cookies | 180 Cal. | (p. 55) |

## WEEK 2

| DAY 8 | | | |
|---|---|---|---|
| BREAKFAST | Low-Carb Quesadilla | 280 Cal. | (p. 25) |
| LUNCH | Spaghetti Squash with Meatballs | 320 Cal. | (p. 31) |
| DINNER | Garlic Parmesan Crusted Pork Chops | 350 Cal. | (p. 43) |
| SNACK / DESSERT | Mocha Mousse | 170 Cal. | (p. 55) |

| DAY 9 | | | |
|---|---|---|---|
| BREAKFAST | Turkey Bacon & Egg Cups | 180 Cal. | (p. 22) |
| LUNCH | Kale & Quinoa Salad | 250 Cal. | (p. 32) |
| DINNER | Creamy Tuscan Garlic Chicken | 350 Cal. | (p. 44) |
| SNACK / DESSERT | Chocolate Chip Cookies | 230 Cal. | (p. 56) |

| DAY 10 | | | |
|---|---|---|---|
| BREAKFAST | Ham & Cheese Roll-Ups | 150 Cal. | (p. 20) |
| LUNCH | Tuna Avocado Sandwich | 260 Cal. | (p. 32) |
| DINNER | Cajun Chicken & Cauliflower Rice | 280 Cal. | (p. 44) |
| SNACK / DESSERT | Matcha Latte | 100 Cal. | (p. 56) |

| DAY 11 | | | |
|---|---|---|---|
| BREAKFAST | Scrambled Eggs with Spinach & Tomatoes | 230 Cal. | (p. 18) |
| LUNCH | Spicy Shrimp Lettuce Wraps | 200 Cal. | (p. 33) |
| DINNER | Sausage & Pepper | 300 Cal. | (p. 45) |
| SNACK / DESSERT | Coconut Protein Truffles | 180 Cal. | (p. 57) |

| DAY 12 | | | |
|---|---|---|---|
| BREAKFAST | Cottage Cheese with Berries & Almonds | 180 Cal. | (p. 17) |
| LUNCH | Zucchini Noodles with Pesto & Chicken | 280 Cal. | (p. 33) |
| DINNER | Teriyaki Salmon | 250 Cal. | (p. 45) |
| SNACK / DESSERT | Apple Cinnamon Muffins | 220 Cal. | (p. 57) |

| DAY 13 | | | |
|---|---|---|---|
| BREAKFAST | Protein Pancakes | 220 Cal. | (p. 20) |
| LUNCH | Asian Chicken Salad | 280 Cal. | (p. 34) |
| DINNER | Coconut Curry Chicken | 380 Cal. | (p. 46) |
| SNACK / DESSERT | Chocolate Mint Protein Bars | 220 Cal. | (p. 58) |

| DAY 14 | | | |
|---|---|---|---|
| BREAKFAST | Burritos | 240 Cal. | (p. 21) |
| LUNCH | Egg Plant & Hummus Wrap | 220 Cal. | (p. 34) |
| DINNER | Pork Tenderloin with Apples & Onions | 280 Cal. | (p. 46) |
| SNACK / DESSERT | Vanilla Ice Cream | 180 Cal. | (p. 58) |

## WEEK 3

| DAY 15 | | | |
|---|---|---|---|
| BREAKFAST | Sausage & Egg Skillet | 280 Cal. | (p. 21) |
| LUNCH | Beef & Vegetable Stir-Fry | 320 Cal. | (p. 35) |
| DINNER | Beef Fajita Bowls | 280 Cal. | (p. 47) |
| SNACK / DESSERT | Vanilla Almond Protein Balls | 160 Cal. | (p. 59) |

| DAY 16 | | | |
|---|---|---|---|
| BREAKFAST | Low-Carb Pizza | 250 Cal. | (p. 22) |
| LUNCH | Turkey & Cranberry Wrap | 280 Cal. | (p. 35) |
| DINNER | Garlic Butter Steak Bites | 320 Cal. | (p. 47) |
| SNACK / DESSERT | Berry Gelatin | 70 Cal. | (p. 59) |
| DAY 17 | | | |
| BREAKFAST | Salmon & Asparagus Frittata | 280 Cal. | (p. 23) |
| LUNCH | Salmon & Avocado Salad | 320 Cal. | (p. 36) |
| DINNER | Thai Coconut Chicken Curry | 330 Cal. | (p. 48) |
| SNACK / DESSERT | Peanut Butter Cups | 210 Cal. | (p. 60) |
| DAY 18 | | | |
| BREAKFAST | Egg Muffins | 120 Cal. | (p. 19) |
| LUNCH | Chicken & Veggie Wrap | 260 Cal. | (p. 36) |
| DINNER | Lemon Dill Baked Cod | 220 Cal. | (p. 48) |
| SNACK / DESSERT | Cinnamon Roll Bites | 180 Cal. | (p. 60) |
| DAY 19 | | | |
| BREAKFAST | Coconut Flour Waffles | 180 Cal. | (p. 23) |
| LUNCH | Baked Cod with Garlic & Herb Butter | 240 Cal. | (p. 37) |
| DINNER | Keto Chicken Alfredo Casserole | 350 Cal. | (p. 49) |
| SNACK / DESSERT | Chocolate Banana Bread | 220 Cal. | (p. 61) |
| DAY 20 | | | |
| BREAKFAST | Almond Butter Protein Bars | 250 Cal. | (p. 24) |
| LUNCH | Egg Plant Lasagna | 380 Cal. | (p. 29) |
| DINNER | Pesto Shrimp Zoodles | 280 Cal. | (p. 49) |
| SNACK / DESSERT | Chocolate Coconut Bars | 220 Cal. | (p. 61) |
| DAY 21 | | | |
| BREAKFAST | Avocado & Smoked Salmon Toast | 300 Cal. | (p. 17) |
| LUNCH | Mediterranean Tuna Salad | 250 Cal. | (p. 37) |
| DINNER | Sausage & Pepper | 300 Cal. | (p. 45) |
| SNACK / DESSERT | Strawberry Protein Cheesecake | 180 Cal. | (p. 54) |

# WEEK 4

| DAY 22 | | | |
|---|---|---|---|
| **BREAKFAST** | Coconut Flour Waffles | 180 Cal. | (p. 23) |
| **LUNCH** | Grilled Chicken & Pesto Wrap | 350 Cal. | (p. 30) |
| **DINNER** | Lemon Garlic Shrimp Pasta | 280 Cal. | (p. 41) |
| **SNACK / DESSERT** | Coconut Lime Protein Balls | 180 Cal. | (p. 52) |
| DAY 23 | | | |
| **BREAKFAST** | Keto Chocolate Chip Pancakes | 250 Cal. | (p. 24) |
| **LUNCH** | Turkey & Cranberry Wrap | 280 Cal. | (p. 35) |
| **DINNER** | Baked Lemon Herb Salmon | 290 Cal. | (p. 40) |
| **SNACK / DESSERT** | Coconut Almond Protein Bites | 180 Cal. | (p. 52) |
| DAY 24 | | | |
| **BREAKFAST** | Cinnamon Roll Mug Cake | 150 Cal. | (p. 25) |
| **LUNCH** | Turkey Avocado Wrap | 280 Cal. | (p. 28) |
| **DINNER** | Balsamic Glazed Chicken | 280 Cal. | (p. 41) |
| **SNACK / DESSERT** | Chocolate Protein Pudding | 180 Cal. | (p. 53) |
| DAY 25 | | | |
| **BREAKFAST** | Greek Yogurt Parfait with Berries & Nuts | 220 Cal. | (p. 16) |
| **LUNCH** | Asian Chicken Salad | 280 Cal. | (p. 34) |
| **DINNER** | Pesto Zoodles with Chicken | 260 Cal. | (p. 42) |
| **SNACK / DESSERT** | Lemon Raspberry Protein Bars | 180 Cal. | (p. 53) |
| DAY 26 | | | |
| **BREAKFAST** | Almond Butter Protein Bars | 250 Cal. | (p. 24) |
| **LUNCH** | Spaghetti Squash with Meatballs | 320 Cal. | (p. 31) |
| **DINNER** | Lamb Chops with Mint Yogurt Sauce | 340 Cal. | (p. 43) |
| **SNACK / DESSERT** | Pumpkin Protein Muffins | 220 Cal. | (p. 54) |
| DAY 27 | | | |
| **BREAKFAST** | Egg Muffins | 120 Cal. | (p. 19) |
| **LUNCH** | Spicy Shrimp Lettuce Wraps | 200 Cal. | (p. 33) |
| **DINNER** | Garlic Butter Shrimp with Asparagus | 280 Cal. | (p. 42) |
| **SNACK / DESSERT** | Mocha Mousse | 170 Cal. | (p. 55) |

| DAY 28 | | | |
|---|---|---|---|
| BREAKFAST | Scrambled Eggs with Spinach & Tomatoes | 230 Cal. | (p. 18) |
| LUNCH | Baked Salmon with Dill & Lemon | 290 Cal. | (p. 29) |
| DINNER | Creamy Tuscan Garlic Chicken | 350 Cal. | (p. 44) |
| SNACK / DESSERT | Peanut Butter Cookies | 180 Cal. | (p. 55) |

## WEEK 5

| DAY 29 | | | |
|---|---|---|---|
| BREAKFAST | Turkey Bacon & Egg Cups | 180 Cal. | (p. 22) |
| LUNCH | Shrimp & Avocado Salad | 280 Cal. | (p. 30) |
| DINNER | Garlic Parmesan Crusted Pork Chops | 350 Cal. | (p. 43) |
| SNACK / DESSERT | Matcha Latte | 100 Cal. | (p. 56) |
| DAY 30 | | | |
| BREAKFAST | Low-Carb Pizza | 250 Cal. | (p. 22) |
| LUNCH | Chicken & Vegetable Skewers | 250 Cal. | (p. 31) |
| DINNER | Teriyaki Salmon | 250 Cal. | (p. 45) |
| SNACK / DESSERT | Chocolate Chip Cookies | 230 Cal. | (p. 56) |
| DAY 31 | | | |
| BREAKFAST | Cinnamon Roll Mug Cake | 150 Cal. | (p. 25) |
| LUNCH | Kale & Quinoa Salad | 250 Cal. | (p. 32) |
| DINNER | Coconut Curry Chicken | 380 Cal. | (p. 46) |
| SNACK / DESSERT | Apple Cinnamon Muffins | 220 Cal. | (p. 57) |
| DAY 32 | | | |
| BREAKFAST | Salmon & Asparagus Frittata | 280 Cal. | (p. 23) |
| LUNCH | Tuna Avocado Sandwich | 260 Cal. | (p. 32) |
| DINNER | Cajun Chicken & Cauliflower Rice | 280 Cal. | (p. 44) |
| SNACK / DESSERT | Coconut Protein Truffles | 180 Cal. | (p. 57) |
| DAY 33 | | | |
| BREAKFAST | Oats with Almond Butter & Bananas | 250 Cal. | (p. 19) |
| LUNCH | Zucchini Noodles with Pesto & Chicken | 280 Cal. | (p. 33) |
| DINNER | Thai Coconut Chicken Curry | 330 Cal. | (p. 48) |
| SNACK / DESSERT | Vanilla Ice Cream | 180 Cal. | (p. 58) |

| DAY 34 | | | |
|---|---|---|---|
| BREAKFAST | Ham & Cheese Roll-Ups | 150 Cal. | (p. 20) |
| LUNCH | Grilled Chicken Caesar Salad | 320 Cal. | (p. 28) |
| DINNER | Garlic Butter Steak Bites | 320 Cal. | (p. 47) |
| SNACK / DESSERT | Vanilla Almond Protein Balls | 160 Cal. | (p. 59) |
| DAY 35 | | | |
| BREAKFAST | Cottage Cheese with Berries & Almonds | 180 Cal. | (p. 17) |
| LUNCH | Egg Plant & Hummus Wrap | 220 Cal. | (p. 34) |
| DINNER | Pork Tenderloin with Apples & Onions | 280 Cal. | (p. 46) |
| SNACK / DESSERT | Chocolate Mint Protein Bars | 220 Cal. | (p. 58) |

## WEEK 6

| DAY 36 | | | |
|---|---|---|---|
| BREAKFAST | Spinach & Feta Omelette | 220 Cal. | (p. 17) |
| LUNCH | Beef & Vegetable Stir-Fry | 320 Cal. | (p. 35) |
| DINNER | Teriyaki Salmon | 250 Cal. | (p. 45) |
| SNACK / DESSERT | Peanut Butter Cups | 210 Cal. | (p. 60) |
| DAY 37 | | | |
| BREAKFAST | Sausage & Egg Skillet | 280 Cal. | (p. 21) |
| LUNCH | Salmon & Avocado Salad | 320 Cal. | (p. 36) |
| DINNER | Beef Fajita Bowls | 280 Cal. | (p. 47) |
| SNACK / DESSERT | Cinnamon Roll Bites | 180 Cal. | (p. 60) |
| DAY 38 | | | |
| BREAKFAST | Salmon & Asparagus Frittata | 280 Cal. | (p. 23) |
| LUNCH | Asian Chicken Salad | 280 Cal. | (p. 34) |
| DINNER | Lemon Dill Baked Cod | 220 Cal. | (p. 48) |
| SNACK / DESSERT | Chocolate Banana Bread | 220 Cal. | (p. 61) |
| DAY 39 | | | |
| BREAKFAST | Cinnamon Roll Mug Cake | 150 Cal. | (p. 25) |
| LUNCH | Chicken & Veggie Wrap | 260 Cal. | (p. 36) |
| DINNER | Keto Chicken Alfredo Casserole | 350 Cal. | (p. 49) |
| SNACK / DESSERT | Berry Gelatin | 70 Cal. | (p. 59) |

| DAY 40 | | | |
|---|---|---|---|
| BREAKFAST | Keto Chocolate Chip Pancakes | 250 Cal. | (p. 24) |
| LUNCH | Baked Cod with Garlic & Herb Butter | 240 Cal. | (p. 37) |
| DINNER | Sausage & Pepper | 300 Cal. | (p. 45) |
| SNACK / DESSERT | Coconut Almond Protein Bites | 180 Cal. | (p. 52) |
| DAY 41 | | | |
| BREAKFAST | Burritos | 240 Cal. | (p. 21) |
| LUNCH | Turkey & Cranberry Wrap | 280 Cal. | (p. 35) |
| DINNER | Grilled Steak with Chimichurri Sauce | 370 Cal. | (p. 40) |
| SNACK / DESSERT | Peanut Butter Cups | 210 Cal. | (p. 60) |
| DAY 42 | | | |
| BREAKFAST | Protein Pancakes | 220 Cal. | (p. 20) |
| LUNCH | Egg Plant Lasagna | 380 Cal. | (p. 29) |
| DINNER | Pesto Shrimp Zoodles | 280 Cal. | (p. 49) |
| SNACK / DESSERT | Chocolate Coconut Bars | 220 Cal. | (p. 61) |

## WEEK 7

| DAY 43 | | | |
|---|---|---|---|
| BREAKFAST | Egg Muffins | 120 Cal. | (p. 19) |
| LUNCH | Baked Salmon with Dill & Lemon | 290 Cal. | (p. 29) |
| DINNER | Balsamic Glazed Chicken | 280 Cal. | (p. 41) |
| SNACK / DESSERT | Pumpkin Protein Muffins | 220 Cal. | (p. 54) |
| DAY 44 | | | |
| BREAKFAST | Greek Yogurt Parfait with Berries & Nuts | 220 Cal. | (p. 16) |
| LUNCH | Mediterranean Tuna Salad | 250 Cal. | (p. 37) |
| DINNER | Lemon Garlic Shrimp Pasta | 280 Cal. | (p. 41) |
| SNACK / DESSERT | Coconut Lime Protein Balls | 180 Cal. | (p. 52) |
| DAY 45 | | | |
| BREAKFAST | Turkey Bacon & Egg Cups | 180 Cal. | (p. 22) |
| LUNCH | Grilled Chicken & Pesto Wrap | 350 Cal. | (p. 30) |
| DINNER | Baked Lemon Herb Salmon | 290 Cal. | (p. 40) |
| SNACK / DESSERT | Chocolate Coconut Bars | 220 Cal. | (p. 61) |

## DAY 46

| BREAKFAST | Coconut Flour Waffles | 180 Cal. | (p. 23) |
|---|---|---|---|
| LUNCH | Egg Plant & Hummus Wrap | 220 Cal. | (p. 34) |
| DINNER | Garlic Butter Shrimp with Asparagus | 280 Cal. | (p. 42) |
| SNACK / DESSERT | Lemon Raspberry Protein Bars | 180 Cal. | (p. 53) |

## DAY 47

| BREAKFAST | Cinnamon Roll Mug Cake | 150 Cal. | (p. 25) |
|---|---|---|---|
| LUNCH | Turkey Avocado Wrap | 280 Cal. | (p. 28) |
| DINNER | Garlic Parmesan Crusted Pork Chops | 350 Cal. | (p. 43) |
| SNACK / DESSERT | Peanut Butter Cookies | 180 Cal. | (p. 55) |

## DAY 48

| BREAKFAST | Almond Butter Protein Bars | 250 Cal. | (p. 24) |
|---|---|---|---|
| LUNCH | Shrimp & Avocado Salad | 280 Cal. | (p. 30) |
| DINNER | Lamb Chops with Mint Yogurt Sauce | 340 Cal. | (p. 43) |
| SNACK / DESSERT | Chocolate Chip Cookies | 230 Cal. | (p. 56) |

## DAY 49

| BREAKFAST | Scrambled Eggs with Spinach & Tomatoes | 230 Cal. | (p. 18) |
|---|---|---|---|
| LUNCH | Spaghetti Squash with Meatballs | 320 Cal. | (p. 31) |
| DINNER | Coconut Curry Chicken | 380 Cal. | (p. 46) |
| SNACK / DESSERT | Mocha Mousse | 170 Cal. | (p. 55) |

## WEEK 8

## DAY 50

| BREAKFAST | Burritos | 240 Cal. | (p. 21) |
|---|---|---|---|
| LUNCH | Zucchini Noodles with Pesto & Chicken | 280 Cal. | (p. 33) |
| DINNER | Creamy Tuscan Garlic Chicken | 350 Cal. | (p. 44) |
| SNACK / DESSERT | Matcha Latte | 100 Cal. | (p. 56) |

## DAY 51

| BREAKFAST | Ham & Cheese Roll-Ups | 150 Cal. | (p. 20) |
|---|---|---|---|
| LUNCH | Spicy Shrimp Lettuce Wraps | 200 Cal. | (p. 33) |
| DINNER | Pork Tenderloin with Apples & Onions | 280 Cal. | (p. 46) |
| SNACK / DESSERT | Apple Cinnamon Muffins | 220 Cal. | (p. 57) |

| DAY 52 | | | |
|---|---|---|---|
| BREAKFAST | Low-Carb Pizza | 250 Cal. | (p. 22) |
| LUNCH | Chicken & Vegetable Skewers | 250 Cal. | (p. 31) |
| DINNER | Garlic Butter Steak Bites | 320 Cal. | (p. 47) |
| SNACK / DESSERT | Chocolate Mint Protein Bars | 220 Cal. | (p. 58) |

| DAY 53 | | | |
|---|---|---|---|
| BREAKFAST | Keto Chocolate Chip Pancakes | 250 Cal. | (p. 24) |
| LUNCH | Kale & Quinoa Salad | 250 Cal. | (p. 32) |
| DINNER | Cajun Chicken & Cauliflower Rice | 280 Cal. | (p. 44) |
| SNACK / DESSERT | Vanilla Ice Cream | 180 Cal. | (p. 58) |

| DAY 54 | | | |
|---|---|---|---|
| BREAKFAST | Spinach & Feta Omelette | 220 Cal. | (p. 17) |
| LUNCH | Tuna Avocado Sandwich | 260 Cal. | (p. 32) |
| DINNER | Beef Fajita Bowls | 280 Cal. | (p. 47) |
| SNACK / DESSERT | Coconut Protein Truffles | 180 Cal. | (p. 57) |

| DAY 55 | | | |
|---|---|---|---|
| BREAKFAST | Sausage & Egg Skillet | 280 Cal. | (p. 21) |
| LUNCH | Beef & Vegetable Stir-Fry | 320 Cal. | (p. 35) |
| DINNER | Thai Coconut Chicken Curry | 330 Cal. | (p. 48) |
| SNACK / DESSERT | Chocolate Protein Pudding | 180 Cal. | (p. 53) |

| DAY 56 | | | |
|---|---|---|---|
| BREAKFAST | Chia Seed Pudding with Almond Milk & Berries | 180 Cal. | (p. 18) |
| LUNCH | Salmon & Avocado Salad | 320 Cal. | (p. 36) |
| DINNER | Keto Chicken Alfredo Casserole | 350 Cal. | (p. 49) |
| SNACK / DESSERT | Vanilla Almond Protein Balls | 160 Cal. | (p. 59) |

## WEEK 9

| DAY 57 | | | |
|---|---|---|---|
| BREAKFAST | Oats with Almond Butter & Bananas | 250 Cal. | (p. 19) |
| LUNCH | Chicken & Veggie Wrap | 260 Cal. | (p. 36) |
| DINNER | Pesto Shrimp Zoodles | 280 Cal. | (p. 49) |
| SNACK / DESSERT | Berry Gelatin | 70 Cal. | (p. 59) |

## DAY 58

| BREAKFAST | Protein Pancakes | 220 Cal. | (p. 20) |
|---|---|---|---|
| LUNCH | Baked Cod with Garlic & Herb Butter | 240 Cal. | (p. 37) |
| DINNER | Lemon Dill Baked Cod | 220 Cal. | (p. 48) |
| SNACK / DESSERT | Chocolate Banana Bread | 220 Cal. | (p. 61) |

## DAY 59

| BREAKFAST | Avocado & Smoked Salmon Toast | 300 Cal. | (p. 17) |
|---|---|---|---|
| LUNCH | Mediterranean Tuna Salad | 250 Cal. | (p. 37) |
| DINNER | Pesto Shrimp Zoodles | 280 Cal. | (p. 49) |
| SNACK / DESSERT | Cinnamon Roll Bites | 180 Cal. | (p. 60) |

## DAY 60

| BREAKFAST | Egg Muffins | 120 Cal. | (p. 19) |
|---|---|---|---|
| LUNCH | Grilled Chicken Caesar Salad | 320 Cal. | (p. 28) |
| DINNER | Pork Tenderloin with Apples & Onions | 280 Cal. | (p. 46) |
| SNACK / DESSERT | Chocolate Coconut Bars | 220 Cal. | (p. 61) |

Embarking on a low-carb, high-protein diet can be a transformative experience for your health and well-being. By following this meal plan and incorporating the flexibility it offers, you can enjoy a wide variety of tasty, easy-to-make, and nutritious meals while achieving your fitness goals. Remember, consistency and balance are key to long-term success.

Stay committed to your health journey and enjoy the benefits of a nutritious, well-balanced diet. Here's to a healthier, stronger, and happier you!

# BONUS CHAPTER:
## CALCULATING YOUR CALORIE NEEDS

## How to Accurately Calculate Your Calorie Needs

Understanding your individual calorie needs is crucial to achieving your health and fitness goals. This chapter will guide you through calculating your daily caloric intake based on various factors such as lifestyle, body size, age, gender, and activity level.

### Step 1: Calculate Your Basal Metabolic Rate (BMR)

Your Basal Metabolic Rate (BMR) represents the number of calories your body needs to maintain basic physiological functions at rest, such as breathing, circulation, and cell production.

BMR Formula for Women:

*BMR = 655 + (9.6 × weight in kg) + (1.8 × height in cm) − (4.7 × age in years)*

BMR Formula for Men:

*BMR = 66 + (13.7 × weight in kg) + (5 × height in cm) − (6.8 × age in years)*

### Step 2: Determine Your Activity Level

Next, determine your daily activity level to adjust your BMR and get your Total Daily Energy Expenditure (TDEE). Here are the activity multipliers based on different levels of physical activity:

> *Sedentary* (little or no exercise): BMR × 1.375
>
> *Moderately active* (moderate exercise/sports 3-5 days a week): BMR × 1.55
>
> *Very active* (hard exercise/sports 6-7 days a week): BMR × 1.725
>
> *Super active* (very hard exercise/sports and a physical job): BMR × 1.9

### Step 3: Calculate Your Total Daily Energy Expenditure (TDEE)

Multiply your BMR by the activity multiplier to get your Total Daily Energy Expenditure (TDEE). This number represents the total calories you need to maintain your current weight.

*TDEE = BMR × Activity Multiplier*

### Step 4: Adjust for Weight Goals

Depending on your goal, you will need to adjust your calorie intake:

> *Weight Loss*: To lose weight, create a calorie deficit by eating fewer calories than your TDEE. A common recommendation is to reduce your intake by 500 calories per day to lose approximately 0.45 kg (1 pound) per week.
>
> *Muscle Gain*: To gain muscle, create a calorie surplus by eating more calories than your TDEE. An additional 250-500 calories per day is typically recommended.

*Example Calculation*

Let's go through an example to illustrate how to calculate your calorie needs.

**Example for a Woman**

- *Weight*: 70 kg

- *Height*: 165 cm

- *Age*: 30 years

- *Activity Level*: Moderately active

Step 1: Calculate BMR

$$BMR = 655 + (9.6 \times 70) + (1.8 \times 165) - (4.7 \times 30)$$
$$BMR = 655 + 672 + 297 - 141$$
$$BMR = 1483 \text{ calories/day}$$

Step 2: Determine Activity Level

Moderately active: $BMR \times 1.55$

Step 3: Calculate TDEE

$$TDEE = 1483 \times 1.55$$
$$TDEE = 2298.65 \text{ calories/day}$$

Step 4: Adjust for Weight Goals

For weight loss:

*2298.65 − 500 = 1798.65 calories/day*

For muscle gain:

*2298.65 + 250 = 2548.65 calories/day*

## Monitoring and Adjusting

Regularly monitor your progress and adjust your calorie intake as needed. Use a food diary or a calorie tracking app to keep track of your daily intake and ensure you're meeting your goals.

# BONUS CHAPTER 2:
## EASY DIETARY SUBSTITUTIONS

Understanding how to substitute ingredients in recipes is essential for accommodating various dietary restrictions or preferences. Whether you follow a paleo, gluten-free, dairy-free, or another specific diet, these tips will help you make appropriate adjustments to your meals while maintaining their flavor and nutritional value.

## Paleo Diet Substitutions

The paleo diet focuses on whole, unprocessed foods similar to what our ancestors might have eaten. Here are some common substitutions:

> *Grains*: Replace grains like rice and pasta with cauliflower rice, zucchini noodles, or spaghetti squash.
>
> *Legumes*: Substitute beans and lentils with additional vegetables or meats.
>
> *Dairy*: Use coconut milk, almond milk, or cashew cheese instead of dairy milk, cheese, or cream.
>
> *Sweeteners*: Opt for natural sweeteners like honey, maple syrup, or coconut sugar instead of refined sugar.

## Gluten-Free Substitutions

A gluten-free diet eliminates all forms of gluten, found in wheat, barley, and rye. Here are some substitutions:

> *Flour*: Use almond flour, coconut flour, or gluten-free all-purpose flour instead of wheat flour.
>
> *Bread*: Replace bread with gluten-free bread, lettuce wraps, or rice paper.
>
> *Pasta*: Choose gluten-free pasta varieties made from rice, quinoa, or chickpeas, or use vegetable noodles.
>
> *Breadcrumbs*: Substitute with gluten-free breadcrumbs, crushed nuts, or seeds.

## Dairy-Free Substitutions

For those who are lactose intolerant or prefer to avoid dairy, here are some alternatives:

> *Milk*: Use almond milk, soy milk, coconut milk, or oat milk instead of cow's milk.
>
> *Cheese*: Replace cheese with dairy-free cheese, nutritional yeast, or homemade nut-based cheese.

*Butter*: Substitute butter with coconut oil, olive oil, or dairy-free margarine.

*Yogurt*: Use coconut yogurt, almond yogurt, or soy yogurt instead of dairy yogurt.

## Vegan Substitutions

A vegan diet excludes all animal products. Here are some substitutions:

*Meat*: Replace meat with tofu, tempeh, seitan, or legumes like beans and lentils.

*Eggs*: Use flaxseed or chia seed gel, applesauce, or mashed bananas as egg substitutes in baking.

*Honey*: Use maple syrup, agave nectar, or date syrup instead of honey.

*Gelatin*: Replace gelatin with agar-agar or pectin.

## Keto Substitutions

For those following a low-carb or ketogenic diet, here are some useful swaps:

*Grains*: Use cauliflower rice, shirataki noodles, or zucchini noodles instead of grains.

*Sugar*: Replace sugar with low-carb sweeteners like stevia, erythritol, or monk fruit sweetener.

*Starches*: Use almond flour, coconut flour, or flaxseed meal instead of starches like corn or potato starch.

*Legumes*: Substitute legumes with more low-carb vegetables or meats.

## General Tips for Substitutions

### *Experiment Gradually*
Start by substituting one ingredient at a time to see how it affects the recipe.

### *Maintain Flavor Balance*
Use herbs, spices, and natural flavor enhancers to maintain the dish's taste.

### *Texture Matters*
Choose substitutes that mimic the texture of the original ingredient to keep the dish's integrity.

### *Read Labels*
Ensure that packaged substitutes align with your dietary needs and preferences.

*Seek Inspiration*

Look for recipes specifically designed for your dietary restriction or preference to learn new substitution techniques.

By mastering these substitution tips, you can adapt almost any recipe to fit your dietary needs or preferences without sacrificing flavor or nutritional value. Enjoy experimenting in the kitchen and discovering new, delicious ways to accommodate your diet!

# MAKING THIS DIET A LIFESTYLE

Transitioning from a diet to a sustainable lifestyle is key to maintaining long-term health and fitness. Here are practical tips on how to support your low-carb, high-protein diet as a permanent part of your routine, manage hunger effectively, ensure balanced meals, and avoid overeating.

## Embracing the Lifestyle

*Set Realistic Goals*: Start with achievable goals that gradually lead to bigger changes. Celebrate small victories to stay motivated.

*Stay Educated*: Continuously learn about nutrition and the benefits of a low-carb, high-protein diet. Knowledge will empower you to make better choices.

## Practical Tips for Sustaining the Diet

*Meal Planning and Prep*: Consistently plan and prepare your meals to avoid last-minute unhealthy choices. Utilize meal prep guides to streamline the process.

*Stock Up on Essentials*: Keep your pantry and fridge stocked with healthy staples like lean proteins, vegetables, nuts, and seeds. This will make it easier to whip up quick, nutritious meals.

## Managing Hunger

*Eat Protein-Rich Foods*: High-protein foods keep you fuller for longer. Include protein in every meal and snack.

*Stay Hydrated*: Sometimes, thirst is mistaken for hunger. Drink plenty of water throughout the day to stay hydrated and help control hunger.

*Fiber-Rich Foods*: Incorporate fiber-rich vegetables and fruits to help manage hunger and support digestive health.

## Ensuring Balanced Meals

*Follow the Plate Method*: Fill half your plate with non-starchy vegetables, a quarter with lean protein, and the remaining quarter with healthy fats or whole grains (if allowed in your diet).

*Mindful Eating*: Pay attention to what you eat and how much you consume. Eat slowly, savor each bite, and listen to your body's hunger and fullness cues.

## Avoiding Overeating

*Regular Meal Times*: Stick to regular meal and snack times to prevent extreme hunger, which can lead to overeating.

*Portion Control*: Be mindful of portion sizes. Use smaller plates and bowls to help control portions and avoid the temptation to overeat.

*Healthy Snacking*: Choose healthy, protein-rich snacks like nuts, seeds, Greek yogurt, or veggie sticks with hummus to keep you satisfied between meals.

## Tips for Long-Term Success

*Variety in Diet*: Keep your meals interesting by trying new recipes and experimenting with different foods. This will prevent boredom and keep you motivated.

*Physical Activity*: Incorporate regular exercise into your routine. It complements your diet and helps you maintain a healthy weight and muscle mass.

*Support System*: Surround yourself with supportive friends, family, or a community who share your health goals. This can provide encouragement and accountability.

## Overcoming Challenges

*Dealing with Cravings*: Acknowledge cravings without guilt. Find healthier alternatives to satisfy your taste buds. For instance, if you crave something sweet, opt for a low-carb, high-protein dessert.

*Eating Out*: When dining out, choose dishes that align with your dietary goals. Don't hesitate to ask for modifications to meet your needs.

*Consistency, Not Perfection*: Strive for consistency rather than perfection. It's okay to have occasional indulgences; what's important is getting back on track.

By integrating these strategies into your daily routine, you can transform your diet into a sustainable lifestyle. This approach will help you feel better, stay fitter, and enjoy the long-term benefits of a healthy, balanced diet.

*Remember...*

*The goal is to create a DIET that you can maintain COMFORTABLY and HAPPILY FOR LIFE!*

# BONUS

# 28-DAY MEAL PLAN

## LOW CARB & HIGH PROTEIN

This plan is perfect for those who want a shorter commitment and an easier, more focused path to achieving their health and fitness goals.

To access your exclusive Bonus Book, use the camera on your mobile phone to *scan the QR code*.

Thank you for choosing the "Low Carb High Protein Cookbook for Beginners." I hope you have enjoyed the recipes and found the meal plans helpful in achieving your health and fitness goals.

If you enjoyed the book, I would greatly appreciate it if you could leave a review on Amazon. Your feedback helps me understand what you loved about the book and allows others to benefit from your experience. Your review can make a difference and support others in their journey to a healthier lifestyle.

Thank you for your support, and happy cooking!

Barbara Grey

Made in the USA
Las Vegas, NV
16 October 2024

96985617R00063